THE
PEARL OF GREA

MW00653888

A SELECTION FROM THE REVELATIONS,
TRANSLATIONS, AND NARRATIONS OF

JOSEPH SMITH

FIRST PROPHET, SEER AND REVELATOR TO
THE CHURCH OF JESUS CHRIST OF
LATTER-DAY SAINTS

———————

PUBLISHED BY
The Church of Jesus Christ of Latter-day Saints
SALT LAKE CITY, UTAH, U. S. A.
1928

First issued, as divided into chapters and verses
with references
By JAMES E. TALMAGE, in
1902

First published in double-column pages,
with index, in
1921

Kessinger Publishing's Rare Reprints
Thousands of Scarce and Hard-to-Find Books!

CONTENTS

THE BOOK OF MOSES

THE BOOK OF ABRAHAM

WRITINGS OF JOSEPH SMITH

THE ARTICLES OF FAITH

ABBREVIATIONS

Books of the Holy Bible are designated by the usual abbreviations.

P. of G. P.........................Pearl of Great Price

The books of the Book of Mormon, some of which are cited in the foot-notes, are designated as follows:

1 Ne.	First Book of Nephi
2 Ne.	Second Book of Nephi
Jac.	Book of Jacob
Enos	Book of Enos
Jar.	Book of Jarom
Om.	Book of Omni
W. of Morm.	The Words of Mormon
Mos.	Book of Mosiah
Al.	Book of Alma
He.	Book of Helaman
3 Ne.	Third Nephi
4 Ne.	Fourth Nephi
Morm.	Book of Mormon
Eth.	Book of Ether
Moro.	Book of Moroni

THE
PEARL OF GREAT PRICE

THE BOOK OF MOSES

CHAPTER 1.

VISIONS OF MOSES

As revealed to Joseph Smith the Prophet, in June, 1830.

1. The words of God, which he spake^a unto Moses at a time when Moses was caught up into an exceedingly high mountain,^b

2. And he saw God^c face to face,^d and he talked with him,^e and the glory of God was upon Moses;^f therefore Moses could endure his presence.^g

3. And God spake unto Moses,^h saying: Behold, I am the Lord God Almighty,ⁱ and Endless^j is my name;^k for I am without beginning of days or end of years;^l and is not this endless?

4. And, behold, thou art my son; wherefore look,^m and I will show thee the workmanship of mine hands;ⁿ but not all, for my works are without end,^o and also my words, for they never cease.^p

5. Wherefore, no man can behold all my works, except he behold all my glory; and no man can behold all my glory, and afterwards remain in the flesh on the earth.^q

6. And I have a work for thee, Moses, my son; and thou art in the similitude of mine Only Begotten;^r and mine Only Begotten^s is and shall be the Savior,^t for he is full of grace and truth;^u but there is no God beside me, and all things are present with me, for I know them all.^v

7. And now, behold, this one

a, vers. 3, 31, 37. 2:1. 4:1, 32. 6:27, 32, 35. 7:32, 41, 60. 8:15. Abraham 1:16. 2:6, 22. 3:4—27. Compare Ex. 31:1. 33:9. Al. 12:30. **b,** ver. 42. **c,** ver. 11. 7:4. See also Ex. 24:10. 33:11. Judg. 13:22. Isa. 6:1—5. Eth. 3. Joseph Smith 2:16—20. D. & C. 76:11—24. 110:1—4. Compare Ex. 3:6. 33:20—23. 1 Ne. 11:11. D. & C. 67:11. **d,** vers. 11, 31. 7:4. Abraham 3:11. Ex. 33:11. Compare Gen. 32:30. Num. 12:8. Judg. 6:22. Al. 38:7. Eth. 12:39. D. & C. 17:1. **e,** Abraham 3:11. Compare D. & C. 17:1. **f,** vers. 11, 18, 25, 31. Compare vers. 9, 14. 3 Ne. 19:25. D. & C. 94:8, 9. See also Moses 7:3, 17. Ex. 33:18. 34:29—35. Matt. 17:2. **g,** vers. 11, 31. Compare ver. 14. **h,** see ver. 1. **i,** ver. 25. 2:1. Compare Ex. 20:2. Lev. 26:1, 13. Deut. 5:6. Ps. 81:10. Hos. 13:4. 2 Ne. 28:15. He. 10:11. 3 Ne. 4:32. **j,** 7:35. Compare 2:1. D. & C. 19:4, 10. **k,** compare 7:35. Abraham 1:16. D. & C. 39:1. **l,** 2:1. 6:67. Compare Abraham 2:8. Isa. 44:6. Rev. 21:6. Mos. 3:5. Al. 11:39. 13:7—9. 3 Ne. 9:18. Moro. 7:22. 8:18. D. & C. 29:33. 39:1. 61:1. 76:4. 88:6—13. 93:8—10. **m,** 7:4, 6, 9, 44, 45. Compare 1 Ne. 11:8, 12, 19. **n,** 7:32, 37. Compare 2 Ne. 27:34. **o,** ver. 38. Compare D. & C. 29:33. **p,** compare 2 Ne. 29. **q,** John 1:18. 1 Tim. 6:16. 1 John 4:12. Compare D. & C. 84:19. Also 35:21. 50:45. 67:10—14. 76:18. 84:88. 93:1. 97:16. 107:19. 110:1. 136:37. **r,** vers. 13, 16. Compare 2:26, 27. Jac. 4:5. Mos. 7:27. Al. 18:34. Eth. 3:6—16. **s,** vers. 17, 21, 32, 33. 2:26, 27. 3:18. 4:28. 5:7, 9, 57. 6:52, 57. 7:50, 59, 62. Compare ver. 19. 5:13. 2 Ne. 25:12. Al. 5:48. 9:26. 13:9. D. & C. 20:21. 29:42. 76:23, 25, 35. 93:11. **t,** compare 5:9. 6:54. 7:39. See also 1 Ne. 10:4. 13:40. 21:26. 22:12. 2 Ne. 6:18. 31:13. Mos. 3:20. 3 Ne. 5:20. Morm. 3:14. 7:10. 8:6. Moro. 8:29. **u,** ver. 32. 5:7. 6:52. 7:11. Compare 2 Ne. 2:6, 8. Al. 5:48. 9:26. 13:9. **v,** ver. 35. 1 Ne. 9:6. W. of Morm. 1:7. Compare Al. 7:13. 40:5, 10. Morm. 8:17.

thing I show unto thee, Moses, my son; for thou art in the world, and now I show it unto thee.

8. And it came to pass that Moses looked, and beheld the world upon which he was created;[w] and Moses beheld the world and the ends thereof, and all the children of men which are, and which were created;[x] of the same he greatly marveled and wondered.

9. And the presence of God[y] withdrew from Moses, that his glory was not upon Moses;[z] and Moses was left unto himself. And as he was left unto himself, he fell unto the earth.[2a]

10. And it came to pass that it was for the space of many hours before Moses did again receive his natural strength like unto man; and he said unto himself: Now, for this cause I know that man is nothing,[2b] which thing I never had supposed.

11. But now mine own eyes have beheld God;[2c] but not my natural,[2d] but my spiritual eyes, for my natural eyes could not have beheld;[2e] for I should have withered and died in his presence;[2f] but his glory was upon me;[2g] and I beheld his face,[2h] for I was transfigured before him.[2i]

12. And it came to pass that when Moses had said these words, behold, Satan[2j] came tempting[2k] him, saying: Moses, son of man,[2l] worship me.[2m]

13. And it came to pass that Moses looked upon Satan[2n] and said: Who art thou? For behold, I am a son of God, in the similitude of his Only Begotten;[2o] and where is thy glory, that I should worship thee?

14. For behold, I could not look upon God, except his glory should come upon me,[2p] and I were strengthened before him.[2q] But I can look upon thee in the natural man.[2r] Is it not so, surely?

15. Blessed be the name of my God, for his Spirit[2s] hath not altogether withdrawn from me, or else where is thy glory, for it is darkness unto me? And I can judge between thee and God;[2t] for God said unto me: Worship God, for him only shalt thou serve.[2u]

16. Get thee hence,[2v] Satan; deceive me not; for God said unto me: Thou art after the similitude of mine Only Begotten.[2w]

17. And he also gave me commandments when he called unto me out of the burning bush,[2x] saying: Call upon God in the name of mine Only Begotten,[2y] and worship me.

18. And again Moses said: I will not cease to call upon God, I have other things to inquire of him: for his glory has been upon me,[2z] wherefore I can judge between him and thee.[3a] Depart hence,[3b] Satan.

w, ver. 27. Compare Abraham 3:11, 12.   **x,** ver. 28. Compare 6:36, 7:21, 23.   **y,** Abraham 2:12.   **z,** compare ver. 2.   **2a,** compare Acts 9:4.   Jac. 7:21. Mos. 4:1. 27:12. Al. 18:42. 22:18. 27:17.   **2b,** compare Job 25:6. **2c,** ver. 2. 1 Ne. 11:11.   **2d,** 6:36. Compare Eth. 12:19. D. & C. 67:10—13. **2e,** compare ver. 14.   **2f,** compare ver. 2.   **2g,** compare ver. 2.   **2h,** compare ver. 2.   **2i,** compare ver. 14.   **2j,** vers. 19, 21. 4:1, 4. 5:13, 18, 21, 29, 30, 38. D. & C. 10:29, 32, 33. 35:24. 43:31. 45:55. 52:14. 63:28. 64:17. 76:28, 29. 101:28. Compare 1 Chron. 21:1. 2 Ne. 2:17. 9:8. 24:12. Mos. 16:3. **2k,** compare 5:38. Matt. 4:1—11.   **2l,** compare 6:57. Ezek. 2:1, 3, 6. Matt. 8:20. D. & C. 49:6.   **2m,** ver. 19. 6:49.   **2n,** compare 7:26. Al. 30:53. D. & C. 76:28.   **2o,** ver. 6.   **2p,** vers. 2, 11.   **2q,** ver. 11.   **2r,** ver. 11.   **2s,** 6:34. 8:17.   **2t,** ver. 18.   **2u,** vers. 17, 20. Compare Ex. 20:3. Deut. 5:7. 6:14. 10:20. Josh. 24:14. 2 Kings 17:35. Jer. 25:6. 35:15. Matt. 4:10. Mos. 12:35. D. & C. 20:19, 29. 133:39.   **2v,** vers. 18, 20, 21, 22. See also Matt. 4:10. **2w,** ver. 6. Compare Rom. 8:29.   **2x,** compare Ex. 3:2.   **2y,** vers. 6, 21, 4:1, 5:8. 6:52.   **2z,** ver. 2.   **3a,** ver. 15.   **3b,** ver. 16.

19. And now, when Moses had said these words, Satan cried with a loud voice, and rent upon the earth, and commanded, saying: I am the Only Begotten,[3c] worship me.[3d]

20. And it came to pass that Moses began to fear exceedingly; and as he began to fear, he saw the bitterness of hell. Nevertheless, calling upon God, he received strength,[3e] and he commanded, saying: Depart from me,[3f] Satan, for this one God only will I worship,[3g] which is the God of glory.

21. And now Satan began to tremble, and the earth shook; and Moses received strength, and called upon God, saying: In the name of the Only Begotten,[3h] depart hence,[3i] Satan.

22. And it came to pass that Satan cried with a loud voice, with weeping, and wailing, and gnashing of teeth;[3j] and he departed hence,[3k] even from the presence of Moses, that he beheld him not.

23. And now of this thing Moses bore record; but because of wickedness it is not had among the children of men.[3l]

24. And it came to pass that when Satan had departed from the presence of Moses, that Moses lifted up his eyes unto heaven, being filled with the Holy Ghost,[3m] which beareth record of the Father and the Son;[3n]

25. And calling upon the name of God, he beheld his glory again,

for it was upon him;[3o] and he heard a voice,[3p] saying: Blessed art thou, Moses, for I, the Almighty,[3q] have chosen[3r] thee, and thou shalt be made stronger than many waters; for they shall obey thy command as if thou wert God.[3s]

26. And lo, I am with thee, even unto the end of thy days; for thou shalt deliver my people from bondage,[3t] even Israel my chosen.[3u]

27. And it came to pass, as the voice[3v] was still speaking, Moses cast his eyes and beheld the earth, yea, even all of it;[3w] and there was not a particle of it which he did not behold, discerning it by the Spirit of God.[3x]

28. And he beheld also the inhabitants thereof,[3y] and there was not a soul which he beheld not; and he discerned them by the Spirit of God;[3z] and their numbers were great, even numberless as the sand upon the sea shore.[4a]

29. And he beheld many lands; and each land was called earth, and there were inhabitants on the face thereof.

30. And it came to pass that Moses called upon God,[4b] saying: Tell me,[4c] I pray thee, why these things are so, and by what thou madest them?

31. And behold, the glory of the Lord was upon Moses,[4d] so that Moses stood in the presence of God,[4e] and talked with him face to face.[4f] And the Lord God

3c, compare 5:13.   3d, ver. 12.   3e, Joseph Smith 2:16.   Compare Al. 36:18—20.   3f, ver. 16.   3g, ver. 15.   3h, ver. 17.   3i, ver. 16.   3j, compare Matt. 8:12.   13:42.   24:51.   Luke 13:28.   Mos. 16:2.   Al. 40:13.   3k, ver. 16.   3l, ver. 41.   3m, 5:9, 14, 58.   6:8, 26, 34, 52, 64, 66.   7:11, 27.   8:24.   Al. 8:30.   36:24.   3 Ne. 12:6.   19:13.   26:17.   30:2.   D. & C. 46:13.   3n, 5:9.   6:66. 7:11, 27.   Compare 1 Ne. 10:10.   12:7.   He. 8:14.   3 Ne. 11:15, 32—36.   3o, ver. 2.   3p, 4:14.   5:4.   6:27, 66.   7:2, 25.   Compare 7:48, 56.   Acts 9:4.   2 Ne. 31:15. He. 5:30.   3 Ne. 9:1.   11:3, 4, 6.   3q, ver. 3.   3r, compare 4:2.   7:39.   Abraham 3:23.   Matt. 20:16.   John 6:70.   15:16.   Acts 9:15.   Eph. 1:4.   1 Pet. 2:4. 1 Ne. 12:7, 8.   Mos. 7:26.   Al. 10:7.   16:15.   He. 9:16.   3 Ne. 12:1.   13:25.   15:11. 18:26, 36.   19:4, 12, 20, 28.   26:17.   28:34, 36.   4 Ne. 14.   Moro. 2:1.   D. & C. 1:4. 19:9.   105:36.   107:40.   3s, compare Ex. 4:16.   7:1.   3t, compare Ex. 3:7—12. 3u, compare ver. 25.   1 Ne. 20:12.   3v, see ver. 25.   3w, ver. 8.   3x, ver. 28 3y, ver. 8.   3z, ver. 27.   4a, compare 7:30.   4b, ver. 36.   6:31, 53, 64.   7:20 54.   Abraham 1:15.   2:6, 17.   4c, ver. 36.   4d, ver. 2.   4e, ver. 2.   4f, ver. 2.

said unto Moses:[4g] For mine own purpose[4h] have I made these things. Here is wisdom and it remaineth in me.

32. And by the word of my power,[4i] have I created them, which is mine Only Begotten Son,[4j] who is full of grace and truth.[4k]

33. And worlds without number have I created; and I also created them for mine own purpose; and by the Son I created them, which is mine Only Begotten.[4l]

34. And the first man of all men[4m] have I called Adam,[4n] which is many.

35. But only an account of this earth, and the inhabitants thereof, give I unto you. For behold, there are many worlds that have passed away[4o] by the word of my power. And there are many that now stand, and innumerable are they unto man;[4p] but all things are numbered unto me, for they are mine and I know them.[4q]

36. And it came to pass that Moses spake unto the Lord,[4r] saying: Be merciful unto thy servant, O God, and tell me[4s] concerning this earth, and the inhabitants thereof, and also the heavens, and then thy servant will be content.

37. And the Lord God spake unto Moses,[4t] saying: The heavens, they are many, and they cannot be numbered unto man; but they are numbered unto me, for they are mine.[4u]

38. And as one earth shall pass away, and the heavens thereof[4v] even so shall another come; and

there is no end to my works, neither to my words.[4w]

39. For behold, this is my work and my glory—to bring to pass the immortality and eternal life of man.[4x]

40. And now, Moses, my son, I will speak unto thee concerning this earth upon which thou standest;[4y] and thou shalt write the things which I shall speak.[4z]

41. And in a day when the children of men shall esteem my words as naught and take many of them from the book which thou shalt write, behold, I will raise up another like unto thee; and they shall be had again among the children of men—among as many as shall believe.[5a]

42. (These words were spoken unto Moses in the mount,[5b] the name of which shall not be known among the children of men. And now they are spoken unto you. Show them not unto any except them that believe.[5c] Even so. Amen.)

CHAPTER 2.[a]

THE WRITINGS OF MOSES

As revealed to Joseph Smith the Prophet, in December, 1830.

1. And it came to pass that the Lord spake[b] unto Moses, saying: Behold, I reveal unto you concerning this heaven, and this earth; write the words which I speak.[c] I am the Beginning and the End,[d] the Almighty God;[e] by mine Only Begotten I created these things;[f] yea, in the beginning I created the heaven, and

4g, ver. 1.   **4h,** compare ver. 33. Jac. 4:9.   Morm. 9:17.   D. & C. 29:30. Compare Mos. 4:2.   D. & C. 76:13.   Abraham 1:3.   **4n,** 6:9, 45.   Abraham 1:3. **4p,** ver. 37.   **4q,** vers. 6, 37.   **4r,** ver. 30. 35.   **4v,** ver. 35.   **4w,** ver. 4.   Compare 2:1. **5a,** compare ver. 23.   **5b,** ver. 1.   **5c,** compare 4:32.   Joseph Smith 2:41. CHAP. 2: **a,** compare verse by verse with Abraham chap. 4, and Gen. chap. 1. **b,** 1:1.   **c,** 1:40.   **d,** compare 1:3.   **e,** 1:3.   **f,** 1:32.
4i, 2:5.   Compare 2:16.   3:7.   4:3. **4j,** ver. 33.   2:1.   4:3.   See also ver. 6. **4k,** ver. 6.   **4l,** see ver. 6.   **4m,** 3:7. 1 Ne. 5:11.   Gen. 2:19.   **4o,** ver. 38. **4s,** ver. 30.   **4t,** ver. 1.   **4u,** ver. **4x,** 6:59.   **4y** 2:1.   **4z,** 2:1.

the earth upon which thou stand-est.[g]

2. And the earth was without form, and void; and I caused darkness to come up upon the face of the deep; and my Spirit moved upon the face of the water; for I am God.

3. And I, God, said: Let there be light; and there was light.

4. And I, God, saw the light; and that light was good.[h] And I, God, divided the light from the darkness.

5. And I, God, called the light Day; and the darkness, I called Night; and this I did by the word of my power,[i] and it was done as I spake; and the evening and the morning were the first day.

6. And again, I, God, said: Let there be a firmament in the midst of the water, and it was so, even as I spake; and I said: Let it divide the waters from the waters; and it was done;

7. And I, God, made the firmament and divided the waters, yea, the great waters under the firmament from the waters which were above the firmament, and it was so even as I spake.

8. And I, God, called the firmament Heaven; and the evening and the morning were the second day.

9. And I, God, said: Let the waters under the heaven be gathered together unto one place, and it was so; and I, God, said: Let there be dry land; and it was so.

10. And I, God, called the dry land Earth; and the gathering together of the waters, called I the Sea; and I, God, saw that all things which I had made were good.[j]

11. And I, God, said: Let the earth bring forth grass, the herb yielding seed, the fruit tree yield-ing fruit, after his kind, and the tree yielding fruit, whose seed should be in itself upon the earth, and it was so even as I spake.

12. And the earth brought forth grass, every herb yielding seed after his kind, and the tree yielding fruit, whose seed should be in itself, after his kind; and I, God, saw that all things which I had made were good;[k]

13. And the evening and the morning were the third day.

14. And I, God, said: Let there be lights in the firmament of the heaven, to divide the day from the night, and let them be for signs, and for seasons, and for days, and for years;

15. And let them be for lights in the firmament of the heaven to give light upon the earth; and it was so.

16. And I, God, made two great lights; the greater light to rule the day, and the lesser light to rule the night, and the greater light was the sun, and the lesser light was the moon; and the stars also were made even according to my word.[l]

17. And I, God, set them in the firmament of the heaven to give light upon the earth,

18. And the sun to rule over the day, and the moon to rule over the night, and to divide the light from the darkness; and I, God, saw that all things which I had made were good;[m]

19. And the evening and the morning were the fourth day.

20. And I, God, said: Let the waters bring forth abundantly the moving creature that hath life, and fowl which may fly above the earth in the open firmament of heaven.

21. And I, God, created great whales, and every living creature

---

g, 1:40.   h, vers. 10, 12, 18, 21, 25, 31.   3:2.   i, 1:32.   j, see ver. 4.
k, see ver. 4.   l, compare 1:32.   m, see ver. 4.

that moveth, which the waters brought forth abundantly, after their kind, and every winged fowl after his kind; and I, God, saw that all things which I had created were good.[n]

22. And I, God, blessed them, saying: Be fruitful, and multiply, and fill the waters in the sea; and let fowl multiply in the earth;

23. And the evening and the morning were the fifth day.

24. And I, God, said: Let the earth bring forth the living creature after his kind, cattle, and creeping things, and beasts of the earth after their kind, and it was so;

25. And I, God, made the beasts of the earth after their kind, and cattle after their kind, and everything which creepeth upon the earth after his kind; and I, God, saw that all these things were good.[o]

26. And I, God, said unto mine Only Begotten,[p] which was with me from the beginning:[q] Let us make man[r] in our image, after our likeness;[s] and it was so. And I, God, said: Let them have dominion[t] over the fishes of the sea, and over the fowl of the air, and over the cattle, and over all the earth, and over every creeping thing that creepeth upon the earth.

27. And I, God, created man in mine own image, in the image of mine Only Begotten created I him;[u] male and female created I them.

28. And I, God, blessed them, and said unto them: Be fruitful, and multiply, and replenish the earth,[v] and subdue it, and have dominion over the fish of the sea,

and over the fowl of the air, and over every living thing that moveth upon the earth.

29. And I, God, said unto man: Behold, I have given you every herb bearing seed, which is upon the face of all the earth, and every tree in the which shall be the fruit of a tree yielding seed; to you it shall be for meat.

30. And to every beast of the earth, and to every fowl of the air, and to everything that creepeth upon the earth, wherein I grant life, there shall be given every clean herb for meat; and it was so, even as I spake.

31. And I, God, saw everything that I had made, and, behold, all things which I had made were very good;[w] and the evening and the morning were the sixth day.

CHAPTER 3.[a]

THE WRITINGS OF MOSES

As revealed to Joseph Smith the Prophet, in December, 1830—Continued.

1.[b] Thus the heaven and the earth were finished, and all the host of them.

2. And on the seventh day I, God, ended my work, and all things which I had made; and I rested on the seventh day from all my work, and all things which I had made were finished, and I, God, saw that they were good;[c]

3. And I, God, blessed the seventh day, and sanctified it; because that in it I had rested from all my work which I, God, had created and made.

4. And now, behold, I say unto you, that these are the generations of the heaven and of the earth, when they were created,

in the day that I, the Lord God, made the heaven and the earth;

5. And every plant of the field before it was in the earth, and every herb of the field before it grew. For I, the Lord God, created all things, of which I have spoken, spiritually,[d] before they were naturally upon the face of the earth. For I, the Lord God, had not caused it to rain upon the face of the earth. And I, the Lord God, had created all the children of men; and not yet a man to till the ground; for in heaven created I them; and there was not yet flesh upon the earth, neither in the water, neither in the air;

6. But I, the Lord God, spake, and there went up a mist from the earth, and watered the whole face of the ground.

7. And I, the Lord God, formed man from the dust of the ground,[e] and breathed into his nostrils the breath of life;[f] and man became a living soul,[g] the first flesh upon the earth, the first man[h] also; nevertheless, all things were before created; but spiritually were they created and made according to my word:[i]

8. And I, the Lord God, planted a garden eastward in Eden,[j] and there I put the man whom I had formed.

9. And out of the ground made I, the Lord God, to grow every tree, naturally,[k] that is pleasant to the sight of man; and man could behold it. And it became also a living soul.[l] For it was spiritual in the day that I created it; for it remaineth in the sphere in which I, God, created it, yea, even all things which I prepared for the use of man; and man saw that it was good for food. And I, the Lord God, planted the tree of life[m] also in the midst of the garden, and also the tree of knowledge of good and evil.[n]

10. And I, the Lord God, caused a river to go out of Eden to water the garden; and from thence it was parted, and became into four heads.

11. And I, the Lord God, called the name of the first Pison, and it compasseth the whole land of Havilah, where I, the Lord God, created much gold;

12. And the gold of that land was good, and there was bdellium and the onyx stone.

13. And the name of the second river was called Gihon; the same that compasseth the whole land of Ethiopia.

14. And the name of the third river was Hiddekel; that which goeth toward the east of Assyria. And the fourth river was the Euphrates.

15.[o] And I, the Lord God, took the man, and put him into the Garden of Eden,[p] to dress it, and to keep it.

16. And I, the Lord God, commanded the man, saying: Of every tree of the garden thou mayest freely eat,

17. But of the tree of the knowledge of good and evil,[q] thou shalt not eat of it,[r] nevertheless, thou mayest choose for thyself,[s] for it is given unto thee; but, remember that I forbid it, for in the day thou eatest thereof thou shalt surely die.[t]

d, vers. 7, 9. 6:51. Abraham 3:23. Compare D. & C. 29:31—34. e, 4:25, 29. 6:59. Compare Mos. 2:25. Morm. 9:17. f, ver. 19. g, vers. 9, 19. 6:9. h, 1:34. Abraham 1:3. Compare 1 Ne. 5:11. i, compare 1:32. j, ver. 15. 4:14, 29, 31. 5:4, 41. 6:53. 7:32. k, ver. 5. l, ver. 7. m, 4:28, 31. Compare Al. 42:5. n, ver. 17. o, compare vers. 15—18 with Abraham 5:11—14, and Gen. 2:15—18. p, see ver. 8. q, ver. 9. r, 4:9. s, compare 4:3. 6:33, 56. 7:32. Compare D. & C. 29:35. 2 Ne. 2:27. 10:23. Al. 13:3. 30:8. He. 14:31. t, 4:9, 17. Abraham 5:13.

18. And I, the Lord God, said unto mine Only Begotten,^{u} that it was not good that the man should be alone; wherefore, I will make an help meet for him.^{v}

19.^{w} And out of the ground I, the Lord God, formed every beast of the field, and every fowl of the air; and commanded that they should come unto Adam, to see what he would call them; and they were also living souls;^{x} for I, God, breathed into them the breath of life, and commanded that whatsoever Adam called every living creature, that should be the name thereof.

20. And Adam gave names to all cattle, and to the fowl of the air, and to every beast of the field; but as for Adam, there was not found an help meet for him.

21.^{y} And I, the Lord God, caused a deep sleep to fall upon Adam; and he slept, and I took one of his ribs and closed up the flesh in the stead thereof;

22. And the rib which I, the Lord God, had taken from man, made I a woman, and brought her unto the man.

23. And Adam said: This I know now is bone of my bones, and flesh of my flesh; she shall be called Woman, because she was taken out of man.

24. Therefore shall a man leave his father and his mother, and shall cleave unto his wife; and they shall be one flesh.

25. And they were both naked, the man and his wife, and were not ashamed.^{z}

CHAPTER 4.

THE WRITINGS OF MOSES

As revealed to Joseph Smith the Prophet, in December, 1830—Continued.

1. And I, the Lord God, spake^a unto Moses, saying: That Satan,^{b} whom thou hast commanded in the name of mine Only Begotten,^{c} is the same which was from the beginning,^{d} and he came before me, saying—Behold, here am I, send me, I will be thy son, and I will redeem all mankind, that one soul shall not be lost, and surely I will do it; wherefore give me thine honor.^{e}

2. But, behold, my Beloved Son,^{f} which was my Beloved and Chosen^g from the beginning,^{h} said unto me—Father, thy will be done, and the glory be thine forever.^{i}

3. Wherefore, because that Satan rebelled against me,^{j} and sought to destroy the agency of man,^{k} which I, the Lord God, had given him, and also, that I should give unto him mine own power; by the power of mine Only Begotten,^{l} I caused that he should be cast down;^{m}

4. And he became Satan,^{n} yea, even the devil, the father of all lies,^{o} to deceive and to blind men, and to lead them captive at his will, even as many as would not hearken unto my voice.^{p}

5.^{q} And now the serpent^r was more subtle than any beast of the field which I, the Lord God, had made.

u, see 1:6.   **v,** ver. 20.   Abraham 5:14.   **w,** compare vers. 19 and 20 with Abraham 5:20, 21, and with Gen. 2:19, 20.   **x,** see ver. 7.   **y,** compare vers. 21—25 with Abraham 5:15—19, and Gen. 2:21—25.   **z,** 4:13, 16, 17, 27. Chap. 4: **a,** 1:1.   **b,** 1:12.   **c,** 1:17.   See also 1:6.   Compare D. & C. 29:36. 76:25, 26.   **d,** 2:26.   Compare 5:24.   **e,** compare Abraham 3:27, 28.   D. & C. 29:36—39.   76:25.   **f,** Joseph Smith 2:17.   Compare Matt. 3:17.   Mark 1:11. Luke 9:35.   3 Ne. 11:7.   **g,** 1:25.   7:39.   **h,** 2:26.   **i,** compare Abraham 3:27. **j,** Abraham 3:28.   **k,** see 3:17.   **l,** 1:32.   See also 1:6.   **m,** D. & C. 29:36, 37. 76:25—27.   **n,** 1:12.   **o,** compare 5:24.   2 Ne. 2:18.   D. & C. 10:25.   93:25. **p,** 5:16, 57.   8:15, 24.   **q,** compare vers. 5—31 with Gen. chap. 3.   **r,** vers. 19, 20.   2 Ne. 2:18.   Mos. 16:3.

6. And Satan put it into the heart of the serpent, (for he had drawn away many after him,[s]) and he sought also to beguile Eve, for he knew not the mind of God, wherefore he sought to destroy the world.

7. And he said unto the woman: Yea, hath God said—Ye shall not eat of every tree of the garden? (And he spake by the mouth of the serpent.)

8. And the woman said unto the serpent: We may eat of the fruit of the trees of the garden;

9. But of the fruit of the tree which thou beholdest in the midst of the garden, God hath said—Ye shall not eat of it, neither shall ye touch it, lest ye die.[t]

10. And the serpent said unto the woman: Ye shall not surely die;

11. For God doth know that in the day ye eat thereof, then your eyes shall be opened,[u] and ye shall be as gods, knowing good and evil.[v]

12. And when the woman saw that the tree was good for food, and that it became pleasant to the eyes, and a tree to be desired to make her wise, she took of the fruit thereof, and did eat, and also gave unto her husband with her, and he did eat.

13. And the eyes of them both were opened,[w] and they knew that they had been naked.[x] And they sewed fig-leaves together and made themselves aprons.

14. And they heard the voice[y] of the Lord God, as they were walking in the garden,[z] in the cool of the day; and Adam and his wife went to hide themselves from the presence of the Lord God amongst the trees of the garden.

15. And I, the Lord God, called unto Adam, and said unto him: Where goest thou?

16. And he said: I heard thy voice in the garden, and I was afraid, because I beheld that I was naked,[2a] and I hid myself.

17. And I, the Lord God, said unto Adam: Who told thee thou wast naked?[2b] Hast thou eaten of the tree whereof I commanded thee that thou shouldst not eat, if so thou shouldst surely die?[2c]

18. And the man said: The woman thou gavest me, and commandedst that she should remain with me, she gave me of the fruit of the tree and I did eat.[2d]

19. And I, the Lord God, said unto the woman: What is this thing which thou hast done? And the woman said: The serpent beguiled me,[2e] and I did eat.

20. And I, the Lord God, said unto the serpent: Because thou hast done this thou shalt be cursed above all cattle, and above every beast of the field; upon thy belly shalt thou go, and dust shalt thou eat all the days of thy life;

21. And I will put enmity between thee and the woman, between thy seed and her seed; and he shall bruise thy head, and thou shalt bruise his heel.[2f]

22. Unto the woman, I, the Lord God, said: I will greatly multiply thy sorrow and thy conception. In sorrow thou shalt bring forth children, and thy desire shall be to thy husband, and he shall rule over thee.

23. And unto Adam, I, the Lord God, said: Because thou hast hearkened unto the voice of thy wife, and hast eaten of the

s, D. & C. 29:36, 37.   t, 3:16, 17. 6:56. Al. 12:31. 42:3.   w, ver. 11. 2b, 3:25.   2c, 3:17.   2d, ver. 12.   u, ver. 13. 5:10.   v, ver. 28. 5:11. x, 3:25.   y, 1:25.   z, 3:8.   2a, 3:25. 2e, vers. 6—11.   2f, compare D. & C. 29:36—38.

fruit of the tree of which I commanded thee, saying—Thou shalt not eat of it,[2g] cursed shall be the ground for thy sake;[2h] in sorrow shalt thou eat of it all the days of thy life.

24. Thorns also, and thistles shall it bring forth to thee, and thou shalt eat the herb of the field.

25. By the sweat of thy face shalt thou eat bread,[2i] until thou shalt return unto the ground— for thou shalt surely die—for out of it wast thou taken:[2j] for dust thou wast,[2k] and unto dust shalt thou return.

26. And Adam called his wife's name Eve, because she was the mother of all living; for thus have I, the Lord God, called the first of all women, which are many.

27. Unto Adam, and also unto his wife, did I, the Lord God, make coats of skins, and clothed them.[2l]

28. And I, the Lord God, said unto mine Only Begotten:[2m] Behold, the man is become as one of us to know good and evil;[2n] and now lest he put forth his hand and partake also of the tree of life,[2o] and eat and live forever,

29. Therefore I, the Lord God, will send him forth[2p] from the Garden of Eden,[2q] to till the ground[2r] from whence he was taken;[2s]

30. For as I, the Lord God, liveth, even so my words cannot return void, for as they go forth out of my mouth they must be fulfilled.[2t]

31. So I drove out the man,[2u] and I placed at the east of the Garden of Eden,[2v] cherubim and a flaming sword,[2w] which turned every way to keep the way of the tree of life.[2x]

32. (And these are the words which I spake unto my servant Moses,[2y] and they are true even as I will; and I have spoken them unto you. See thou show them unto no man, until I command you, except to them that believe.[2z] Amen.[3a])

CHAPTER 5.

THE WRITINGS OF MOSES

As revealed to Joseph Smith the Prophet, in December, 1830—Continued.

1. And it came to pass that after I, the Lord God, had driven them out,[a] that Adam began to till the earth,[b] and to have dominion[c] over all the beasts of the field, and to eat his bread by the sweat of his brow,[d] as I the Lord had commanded him. And Eve, also, his wife, did labor with him.

2. And Adam knew his wife, and she bare unto him sons and daughters, and they began to multiply and to replenish the earth.[e]

3. And from that time forth, the sons and daughters of Adam began to divide two and two in the land, and to till the land, and to tend flocks, and they also begat sons and daughters.

4. And Adam and Eve, his wife, called upon the name of the Lord, and they heard the voice[f] of the Lord from the way toward the Garden of Eden,[g] speaking unto them, and they saw him not; for they were shut out from his presence.[h]

5. And he gave unto them com-

2g, 3:17.   2h, compare 5:37.   2i, 5:1.   2j, 3:7.   2k, 3:7.   2l, 3:25. 2m, see 1:16.   2n, ver. 11.   2o, ver. 31.   3:9. Compare Al. 42:5.   2p, ver. 31. 5:1.   2q, 3:8.   2r, 5:1.   2s, 3:7.   2t, 5:15.   2u, ver. 29. Compare 2 Ne. 2:19. Al. 42:2.   2v, 3:8.   2w, compare Al. 12:21.   42:2.   2x, 3:9.   Compare Al. 42:2.   2y, 1:1.   2z, see 1:42.   3a, compare vers. 5—31 with Gen. chap. 3. CHAP. 5:   a, 4:29.   b, 4:29.   c, 2:26.   d, 4:25.   e, 2:28.   f, 1:25. g, 3:8.   h, 4:29.

mandments,[i] that they should worship the Lord their God, and should offer the firstlings of their flocks,[j] for an offering unto the Lord. And Adam was obedient unto the commandments of the Lord.

6. And after many days an angel[k] of the Lord appeared unto Adam, saying: Why dost thou offer sacrifices unto the Lord? And Adam said unto him: I know not, save the Lord commanded me.[l]

7. And then the angel spake, saying: This thing is a similitude of the sacrifice of the Only Begotten[m] of the Father, which is full of grace and truth.[n]

8. Wherefore, thou shalt do all that thou doest in the name of the Son,[o] and thou shalt repent[p] and call upon God in the name of the Son forevermore.

9. And in that day the Holy Ghost[q] fell upon Adam, which beareth record of the Father and the Son,[r] saying: I am the Only Begotten[s] of the Father from the beginning,[t] henceforth and forever, that as thou hast fallen thou mayest be redeemed,[u] and all mankind, even as many as will.[v]

10. And in that day Adam blessed God and was filled, and began to prophesy[w] concerning all the families of the earth, saying: Blessed be the name of God, for because of my transgression my eyes are opened,[x] and in this life I shall have joy, and again in the flesh I shall see God.

11. And Eve, his wife, heard all these things and was glad, saying: Were it not for our transgression we never should have had seed,[y] and never should have known good and evil,[z] and the joy of our redemption,[2a] and the eternal life which God giveth unto all the obedient.

LOL

12. And Adam and Eve blessed the name of God, and they made all things known unto their sons and their daughters.

13. And Satan[2b] came among them, saying: I am also a son of God;[2c] and he commanded them, saying: Believe it not; and they believed it not, and they loved Satan more than God.[2d] And men began from that time forth to be carnal, sensual, and devilish.[2e]

14. And the Lord God called upon men by the Holy Ghost[2f] everywhere and commanded them that they should repent;[2g]

15. And as many as believed in the Son, and repented of their sins, should be saved;[2h] and as many as believed not and repented not, should be damned;[2i] and the words went forth out of the mouth of God in a firm decree; wherefore they must be fulfilled.[2j]

16.[2k] And Adam and Eve, his wife,[2l] ceased not to call upon God. And Adam knew Eve his wife, and she conceived and bare Cain, and said: I have gotten a man from the Lord; wherefore he may not reject his words. But behold, Cain hearkened not,[2m] saying: Who is the Lord, that I should know him?

17. And she again conceived and bare his brother Abel. And

---

i, ver. 6. 6:28.   j, ver. 20.   k, ver. 58. See also 7:25, 27.   l, ver. 5. m, compare 1:6.   n, see 1:6.   o, 1:17.   p, ver. 14. 6:1, 23, 27, 50, 57. 7:10, 12. 8:20, 24. Compare 5:25. 6:29. 8:17. D. & C. 3:20.   q, see 1:24.   r, see 1:24.   s, 1:6.   t, 2:26.   u, ver. 11.   v, see 3:17. 4:3.   w, 6:13, 23, 27. 7:2. 8:16.   x, 4:11.   y, compare 2 Ne. 2:22—25.   z, 4:11.   2a, ver. 9. 2b, 1:12. See also 6:49.   2c, 1:19.   2d, vers. 18, 28. Compare 6:15.   2e, 6:49. Compare Mos. 16:3. Al. 42:10. D. & C. 20:20.   2f, see 1:24.   2g, ver. 8. 2h, ver. 9.   2i, compare Mark 16:16. D. & C. 42:60. 68:9. 84:74. 112:29. 2j, 4:30.   2k, compare vers. 16—23 with Gen. 4:1—7.   2l, ver. 4.   2m, see 4:4.

Abel hearkened unto the voice of the Lord.[2n]   And Abel was a keeper of sheep, but Cain was a tiller of the ground.

18. And Cain loved Satan more than God.[2o]   And Satan commanded him, saying: Make an offering unto the Lord.[2p]

19. And in process of time it came to pass that Cain brought of the fruit of the ground an offering unto the Lord.

20. And Abel he also brought of the firstlings of his flock,[2q] and of the fat thereof. And the Lord had respect unto Abel, and to his offering;[2r]

21. But unto Cain, and to his offering, he had not respect. Now Satan knew this, and it pleased him.[2s]   And Cain was very wroth, and his countenance fell.

22. And the Lord said unto Cain: Why art thou wroth? Why is thy countenance fallen?

23. If thou doest well, thou shalt be accepted. And if thou doest not well, sin lieth at the door, and Satan desireth to have thee; and except thou shalt hearken unto my commandments, I will deliver thee up, and it shall be unto thee according to his desire. And thou shalt rule over him;

24. For from this time forth thou shalt be the father of his lies;[2t] thou shalt be called Perdition;[2u] for thou wast also before the world.[2v]

25. And it shall be said in time to come—That these abominations were had from Cain; for he rejected the greater counsel which was had from God; and this is a cursing[2w] which I will put upon thee, except thou repent.[2x]

26. And Cain was wroth,[2y] and listened not any more to the voice of the Lord, neither to Abel, his brother, who walked in holiness before the Lord.[2z]

27. And Adam and his wife mourned before the Lord, because of Cain and his brethren.

28. And it came to pass that Cain took one of his brothers' daughters to wife, and they loved Satan more than God.[3a]

29. And Satan said unto Cain: Swear unto me[3b] by thy throat, and if thou tell it thou shalt die; and swear thy brethren by their heads, and by the living God, that they tell it not; for if they tell it, they shall surely die; and this that thy father may not know it; and this day I will deliver thy brother Abel into thine hands.[3c]

30. And Satan sware unto Cain that he would do according to his commands. And all these things were done in secret.[3d]

31. And Cain said: Truly I am Mahan, the master of this great secret, that I may murder[3e] and get gain. Wherefore Cain was called Master Mahan,[3f] and he gloried in his wickedness.

32. And Cain went into the field, and Cain talked with Abel, his brother. And it came to pass that while they were in the field, Cain rose up against Abel, his brother, and slew him.[3g]

33. And Cain gloried in that which he had done, saying: I am free; surely the flocks of my brother falleth into my hands.

    2n, 6:1. 8:13. Compare ver. 23.   2o, ver. 13.   2p, compare ver. 5.
2q, ver. 5. Compare D. & C. 84:16.   2r, 6:3.   2s, compare 7:26.   2t, 4:4.
2u, compare John 17:12. 2 Thess. 2:3. D. & C. 76:26. See also D. & C. 76:32,
33, 34, 38, 43, 44. 3 Ne. 27:32. 29:7.   2v, compare 4:1.   2w, ver. 36.
2x, compare ver. 8.   2y, compare ver. 21.   2z, ver. 17.   3a, ver. 13.
3b, vers. 49, 52. Compare 6:29. He. 6:27. Eth. 8:9, 15.   3c, ver. 32.   3d, vers.
49, 51. 6:15. Compare He. 6:27. Eth. 8:15.   3e, Eth. 8:15.   3f, ver. 49.
3g, compare Gen. 4:8. D. & C. 84:16.

34.[3h] And the Lord said unto Cain: Where is Abel, thy brother? And he said: I know not. Am I my brother's keeper?

35. And the Lord said: What hast thou done? The voice of thy brother's blood cries unto me from the ground.

36. And now thou shalt be cursed[3i] from the earth which hath opened her mouth to receive thy brother's blood from thy hand.

37. When thou tillest the ground it shall not henceforth yield unto thee her strength.[3j] A fugitive and a vagabond shalt thou be in the earth.[3k]

38. And Cain said unto the Lord:[3l] Satan tempted me[3m] because of my brother's flocks. And I was wroth also; for his offering thou didst accept and not mine;[3n] my punishment is greater than I can bear.

39. Behold thou hast driven me out this day from the face of the Lord, and from thy face shall I be hid;[3o] and I shall be a fugitive and a vagabond in the earth; and it shall come to pass, that he that findeth me will slay me, because of mine iniquities, for these things are not hid from the Lord.

40. And I the Lord said unto him: Whosoever slayeth thee, vengeance shall be taken on him sevenfold.[3p] And I the Lord set a mark upon Cain, lest any finding him should kill him.

41. And Cain was shut out from the presence of the Lord,[3q] and with his wife and many of his brethren dwelt in the land of Nod, on the east of Eden.[3r]

42. And Cain knew his wife, and she conceived and bare Enoch, and he also begat many sons and daughters. And he builded a city, and he called the name of the city after the name of his son, Enoch.

43. And unto Enoch was born Irad, and other sons and daughters. And Irad begat Mahujael, and other sons and daughters. And Mahujael begat Methusael, and other sons and daughters. And Methusael begat Lamech.

44. And Lamech took unto himself two wives; the name of one being Adah, and the name of the other, Zillah.

45. And Adah bare Jabal; he was the father of such as dwell in tents, and they were keepers of cattle; and his brother's name was Jubal, who was the father of all such as handle the harp and organ.

46. And Zillah, she also bare Tubal Cain, an instructor of every artificer in brass and iron. And the sister of Tubal Cain was called Naamah.

47. And Lamech said unto his wives, Adah and Zillah: Hear my voice, ye wives of Lamech, hearken unto my speech; for I have slain a man to my wounding, and a young man to my hurt.

48. If Cain shall be avenged sevenfold,[3s] truly Lamech shall be seventy and seven fold;[3t]

49. For Lamech having entered into a covenant with Satan,[3u] after the manner of Cain, wherein he became Master Mahan,[3v] master of that great secret which was administered unto Cain by Satan; and Irad,[3w] the son of Enoch, having known their secret, began to reveal it unto the sons of Adam;

3h, compare vers. 34—48 with Gen. 4:9—24, verse by verse.   3i, ver. 25. 3j, compare 4:23.   3k, ver. 39.   3l, compare 1:30.   3m, compare ver. 29. See also 1:12.   3n, vers. 20, 21.   3o, ver. 41. 6:49.   3p, ver. 48.   3q, ver. 39.   See also 6:49.   3r, 3:8.   3s, ver. 40.   3t, compare vers. 34—48 with Gen. 4:9—24, verse by verse.   3u, ver. 29.   3v, ver. 31.   3w, ver. 43.

50. Wherefore Lamech, being angry, slew him, not like unto Cain, his brother Abel,[3x] for the sake of getting gain, but he slew him for the oath's sake.

51. For, from the days of Cain, there was a secret combination,[3y] and their works were in the dark, and they knew every man his brother.

52. Wherefore the Lord cursed Lamech, and his house, and all them that had covenanted with Satan;[3z] for they kept not the commandments of God, and it displeased God, and he ministered not unto them, and their works were abominations, and began to spread among all the sons of men.[4a]

53. And it was among the sons of men, and among the daughters of men these things were not spoken, because that Lamech had spoken the secret unto his wives, and they rebelled against him, and declared these things abroad, and had not compassion;

54. Wherefore Lamech was despised, and cast out, and came not among the sons of men, lest he should die.

55. And thus the works of darkness began to prevail among all the sons of men.

56. And God cursed the earth with a sore curse, and was angry with the wicked, with all the sons of men whom he had made;

57. For they would not hearken unto his voice,[4b] nor believe on his Only Begotten Son,[4c] even him whom he declared should come in the meridian of time,[4d] who was prepared from before the foundation of the world.[4e]

58. And thus the Gospel[4f] began to be preached, from the beginning, being declared by holy angels[4g] sent forth from the presence of God, and by his own voice, and by the gift of the Holy Ghost.[4h]

59. And thus all things were confirmed unto Adam, by an holy ordinance, and the Gospel[4i] preached, and a decree sent forth, that it should be in the world, until the end thereof; and thus it was. Amen.

CHAPTER 6.

THE WRITINGS OF MOSES

As revealed to Joseph Smith the Prophet, in December, 1830—Continued.

1. And Adam hearkened unto the voice of God,[a] and called upon his sons to repent.[b]

2.[c] And Adam knew his wife again, and she bare a son, and he called his name Seth. And Adam glorified the name of God; for he said: God hath appointed me another seed, instead of Abel, whom Cain slew.[d]

3. And God revealed himself unto Seth, and he rebelled not, but offered an acceptable sacrifice, like unto his brother Abel.[e] And to him also was born a son, and he called his name Enos.

4. And then began these men to call upon the name of the Lord, and the Lord blessed them;[f]

5. And a book of remembrance[g] was kept, in the which was recorded, in the language of Adam, for it was given unto as many as called upon God to write by the spirit of inspiration;

6. And by them their children

3x, vers. 32, 38.   3y, ver. 30.   3z, ver. 29.   4a, vers. 54—56.   6:15. 8:14, 15, 20.   4b, ver. 16.   Compare 4:4.   4c, see 1:6.   4d, 6:57, 62. 7:46. See also D. & C. 20:26. 39:3.   4e, 2:26.   4f, ver. 59. 8:19. Abraham 2:10, 11. 4g, ver. 6.   4h, see 1:24.   4i, see ver. 58.   CHAP. 6:   a, 5:17.   b, see 5:8. c, compare vers. 2, 3 and 4 with Gen. 4:25, 26.   d, 5:32.   e, 5:20.   f, compare vers. 2, 3 and 4 with Gen. 4:25, 26.   g, ver. 46. Compare Abraham 1:31. 3 Ne. 24:16. Eth. 8:9. D. & C. 85:7—9.

were taught to read and write, having a language which was pure and undefiled.

7. Now this same Priesthood,[h] which was in the beginning, shall be in the end of the world also.[i]

8. Now this prophecy Adam spake, as he was moved upon by the Holy Ghost,[j] and a genealogy was kept of the children of God.[k] And this was the book of the generations of Adam, saying: In the day that God created man, in the likeness of God made he him;

9. In the image of his own body, male and female, created he them,[l] and blessed them, and called their name Adam,[m] in the day when they were created and became living souls[n] in the land upon the footstool of God.[o]

10.[p] And Adam lived one hundred and thirty years, and begat a son in his own likeness, after his own image, and called his name Seth.

11. And the days of Adam, after he had begotten Seth, were eight hundred years, and he begat many sons and daughters;

12. And all the days that Adam lived were nine hundred and thirty years, and he died.

13. Seth lived one hundred and five years, and begat Enos, and prophesied[q] in all his days, and taught his son Enos in the ways of God; wherefore Enos prophesied also.

14. And Seth lived, after he begat Enos, eight hundred and seven years, and begat many sons and daughters.

15. And the children of men[r] were numerous upon all the face of the land. And in those days Satan had great dominion among men,[s] and raged in their hearts; and from thenceforth came wars and bloodshed; and a man's hand was against his own brother,[t] in administering death, because of secret works,[u] seeking for power.

16. All the days of Seth were nine hundred and twelve years, and he died.

17. And Enos lived ninety years, and begat Cainan. And Enos and the residue of the people of God came out from the land, which was called Shulon, and dwelt in a land of promise, which he called after his own son, whom he had named Cainan.[v]

18. And Enos lived, after he begat Cainan, eight hundred and fifteen years, and begat many sons and daughters. And all the days of Enos were nine hundred and five years, and he died.

19. And Cainan lived seventy years, and begat Mahalaleel; and Cainan lived after he begat Mahalaleel eight hundred and forty years, and begat sons and daughters. And all the days of Cainan were nine hundred and ten years, and he died.

20. And Mahalaleel lived sixty-five years, and begat Jared; and Mahalaleel lived, after he begat Jared, eight hundred and thirty years, and begat sons and daughters. And all the days of Mahalaleel were eight hundred and ninety-five years, and he died.

21. And Jared lived one hundred and sixty-two years, and begat Enoch;[w] and Jared lived, after he begat Enoch, eight hun-

h, 8:19. Abraham 1:2, 4, 18, 26, 27, 31. 2:9, 11. Compare Al. 13:1—19. D. & C. 2:1. 67:10. 84:6, 17, 18, 19, 25. i, ver. 30. j, see 1:24. k, 7:1. 8:13. Compare ver. 68. 8:13, 21. Moro. 7:48. D. & C. 11:30. 34:3. 39:4. 42:52. 45:8. 76:58. 128:23. l, see 2:26. m, 1:34. n, 3:7. o, ver. 44. Abraham 2:7 Matt. 5:35. 1 Ne. 17:39. 3 Ne. 12:35. p, compare vers. 10—25 with Gen. 5:3—21. q, 5:10. r, 5:52. s, 5:13. t, 7:33. u, 5:30. v, ver. 41. Compare 7:6, 7. w, vers. 25—68. 7:1—69. 8:1. Compare Gen. 5:19—24. Jude 14, 15. D. & C. 76:57, 67, 100. 84:15. 107:48, 49, 53. 133:54.

dred years, and begat sons and daughters. And Jared taught Enoch in all the ways of God.[x]

22. And this is the genealogy of the sons of Adam, who was the son of God, with whom God, himself, conversed.

23. And they were preachers of righteousness, and spake and prophesied,[y] and called upon all men, everywhere, to repent;[z] and faith was taught unto the children of men.

24. And it came to pass that all the days of Jared were nine hundred and sixty-two years, and he died.

25.[2a] And Enoch lived sixty-five years, and begat Methuselah.[2b]

26. And it came to pass that Enoch journeyed in the land, among the people; and as he journeyed, the Spirit of God descended out of heaven, and abode upon him.[2c]

27. And he heard a voice[2d] from heaven, saying: Enoch, my son, prophesy[2e] unto this people, and say unto them—Repent,[2f] for thus saith the Lord: I am angry with this people, and my fierce anger is kindled against them;[2g] for their hearts have waxed hard, and their ears are dull of hearing, and their eyes cannot see afar off;

28. And for these many generations, ever since the day that I created them, have they gone astray, and have denied me, and have sought their own counsels in the dark; and in their own abominations have they devised murder, and have not kept the commandments, which I gave unto their father, Adam.[2h]

29. Wherefore, they have foresworn themselves, and, by their oaths,[2i] they have brought upon themselves death; and a hell[2j] I have prepared for them, if they repent not;[2k]

30. And this is a decree, which I have sent forth in the beginning of the world, from my own mouth, from the foundation thereof, and by the mouths of my servants, thy fathers, have I decreed it, even as it shall be sent forth in the world, unto the ends thereof.[2l]

31. And when Enoch had heard these words, he bowed himself to the earth, before the Lord, and spake before the Lord,[2m] saying: Why is it that I have found favor in thy sight, and am but a lad, and all the people hate me; for I am slow of speech;[2n] wherefore am I thy servant?

32. And the Lord said[2o] unto Enoch: Go forth and do as I have commanded thee, and no man shall pierce thee. Open thy mouth, and it shall be filled,[2p] and I will give thee utterance, for all flesh is in my hands, and I will do as seemeth me good.

33. Say unto this people: Choose[2q] ye this day, to serve the Lord God who made you.

34. Behold my Spirit is upon you,[2r] wherefore all thy words will I justify; and the mountains shall flee before you,[2s] and the rivers shall turn from their course;[2t] and thou shalt abide in me, and I in you; therefore walk with me.[2u]

x, ver. 41.   **y,** 5:10.   **z,** 5:8.   **2a,** compare vers. 10—25 with Gen. 5:3—21. **2b,** 8:2—7. Compare Gen. 5:21—27. D. & C. 107:50, 53.   **2c,** compare 1:24. **2d,** 1:25.   **2e,** 5:10.   **2f,** 5:8.   **2g,** 7:34. 8:15.   **2h,** 5:5.   **2i,** 5:29.   **2j,** 1:20. Compare 7:37. 1 Ne. 15:35. D. & C. 29:38. 63:4. 76:84, 106.   **2k,** compare 5:8. **2l,** ver. 7.   **2m,** 1:30.   **2n,** compare Ex. 4:10.   **2o,** 1:1.   **2p,** compare 7:13. Ex. 4:12, 15. Matt. 10:19. Mark 13:11. Luke 12:11. D. & C. 33:8—10.   **2q,** 3:17. **2r,** compare 1:15, 24. 8:17.   **2s,** compare Matt. 17:20. Mark 11:23, 24. Jac. 4:6. Eth. 12:30. D. & C. 133:40, 44.   **2t,** 7:13,   **2u,** ver. 39. 7:69. 8:27. Compare Gen. 5:24. 6:9. 17:1.

35. And the Lord spake unto Enoch,[2v] and said unto him: Anoint thine eyes with clay, and wash them, and thou shalt see. And he did so.

36. And he beheld the spirits that God had created;[2w] and he beheld also things which were not visible to the natural eye;[2x] and from thenceforth came the saying abroad in the land: A seer[2y] hath the Lord raised up unto his people.

37. And it came to pass that Enoch went forth in the land, among the people, standing upon the hills and the high places, and cried with a loud voice, testifying against their works; and all men were offended because of him.

38. And they came forth to hear him, upon the high places, saying unto the tent-keepers: Tarry ye here and keep the tents, while we go yonder to behold the seer,[2z] for he prophesieth, and there is a strange thing in the land; a wild man hath come among us.

39. And it came to pass when they heard him, no man laid hands on him; for fear came on all them that heard him; for he walked with God.[3a]

40. And there came a man unto him, whose name was Mahijah, and said unto him: Tell us plainly who thou art, and from whence thou comest?

41. And he said unto them: I came out from the land of Cainan,[3b] the land of my fathers, a land of righteousness unto this day. And my father taught me in all the ways of God.[3c]

42. And it came to pass, as I journeyed from the land of Cainan, by the sea east, I beheld a vision; and lo, the heavens I saw, and the Lord spake with me, and gave me commandment; wherefore, for this cause, to keep the commandment, I speak forth these words.[3d]

43. And Enoch continued his speech, saying: The Lord which spake with me, the same is the God of heaven, and he is my God, and your God, and ye are my brethren, and why counsel ye yourselves, and deny the God of heaven?

44. The heavens he made; the earth is his footstool;[3e] and the foundation thereof is his. Behold, he laid it, an host of men hath he brought in upon the face thereof.

45. And death hath come upon our fathers; nevertheless we know them, and cannot deny, and even the first of all we know, even Adam.[3f]

46. For a book of remembrance[3g] we have written among us, according to the pattern given by the finger of God; and it is given in our own language.

47. And as Enoch spake forth the words of God, the people trembled, and could not stand in his presence.

48. And he said unto them: Because that Adam fell, we are;[3h] and by his fall came death; and we are made partakers of misery and woe.

49. Behold Satan hath come[3i] among the children of men, and tempteth them to worship him;[3j] and men have become earnal, sensual, and devilish,[3k] and are shut out from the presence of God.[3l]

50. But God hath made known

unto our fathers that all men must repent.[3m]

51. And he called upon our father Adam by his own voice, saying: I am God; I made the world, and men before they were in the flesh.[3n]

52. And he also said unto him: If thou wilt turn unto me, and hearken unto my voice, and believe, and repent[3o] of all thy transgressions, and be baptized,[3p] even in water, in the name of mine Only Begotten Son,[3q] who is full of grace and truth,[3r] which is Jesus Christ,[3s] the only name[3t] which shall be given under heaven, whereby salvation shall come unto the children of men, ye shall receive the gift of the Holy Ghost,[3u] asking all things in his name,[3v] and whatsoever ye shall ask, it shall be given you.

53. And our father Adam spake unto the Lord,[3w] and said: Why is it that men must repent and be baptized in water? And the Lord said unto Adam: Behold I have forgiven thee thy transgression in the Garden of Eden.[3x]

54. Hence came the saying abroad among the people, That the Son of God hath atoned for original guilt,[3y] wherein the sins of the parents cannot be answered upon the heads of the children, for they are whole from the foundation of the world.

55. And the Lord spake unto Adam, saying: Inasmuch as thy children are conceived in sin,[3z] even so when they begin to grow up, sin conceiveth in their hearts, and they taste the bitter, that they may know to prize the good.[4a]

56. And it is given unto them to know good from evil;[4b] wherefore they are agents unto themselves,[4c] and I have given unto you another law and commandment.

57. Wherefore teach it unto your children, that all men, everywhere, must repent,[4d] or they can in nowise inherit the kingdom of God, for no unclean thing can dwell there, or dwell in his presence; for, in the language of Adam, Man of Holiness[4e] is his name, and the name of his Only Begotten[4f] is the Son of Man,[4g] even Jesus Christ,[4h] a righteous Judge, who shall come in the meridian of time.[4i]

58. Therefore I give unto you a commandment, to teach these things freely unto your children, saying:

59. That by reason of transgression cometh the fall, which fall bringeth death, and inasmuch as ye were born into the world by water, and blood, and the spirit, which I have made, and so became of dust a living soul,[4j] even so ye must be born again[4k] into the kingdom of heaven, of water, and of the Spirit,[4l] and be cleansed by blood, even the blood of mine Only Begotten;[4m] that ye might be sanctified from all sin, and enjoy the words of eternal life in this world, and eternal life in the world to come, even immortal glory;[4n]

60. For by the water ye keep the commandment; by the Spirit

3m, 5:8.   3n, 3:5.   3o, see 5:8.   3p, vers. 64, 65. 7:11. 8:24. Compare Matt. 28:19. 3 Ne. 11:23.   3q, 1:6, 17.   3r, 1:6.   3s, ver. 57. 7:50. 8:24. 3t, compare 2 Ne. 25:20. Mos. 3:17. 5:8. D. & C. 76:1.   3u, see 1:24.   3v, compare Jac. 4:6. 3 Ne. 7:19, 20. 8:1. 19:6—8. 26:17, 21. 28:30. 4 Ne. 5. Morm. 9:6, 27. Eth. 5:5. D. & C. 46:31.   3w, 1:30.   3x, 3:8.   3y, compare 1:6. 5:9.   3z, Ps. 51:5.   4a, compare D. & C. 29:39.   4b, 4:11.   4c, 3:17. 4d, 5:8.   4e, 7:35.   4f, 1:6.   4g, 7:24, 47, 54. Compare 1:12.   4h, ver. 52. 4i, see 5:57.   4j, 3:7.   4k, compare 6:65. John 3:3—5. Mos. 27:25. Al. 5:49. 7:14.   4l, ver. 64.   4m, 1:6.   4n, compare 1:39.

ye are justified, and by the blood ye are sanctified;

61. Therefore it is given to abide in you; the record of heaven; the Comforter;[40] the peaceable things of immortal glory; the truth of all things; that which quickeneth all things, which maketh alive all things; that which knoweth all things, and hath all power, according to wisdom, mercy, truth, justice, and judgment.

62. And now, behold, I say unto you: This is the plan of salvation unto all men, through the blood of mine Only Begotten,[4p] who shall come in the meridian of time.[4q]

63. And behold, all things have their likeness, and all things are created and made to bear record of me, both things which are temporal, and things which are spiritual; things which are in the heavens above, and things which are on the earth, and things which are in the earth, and things which are under the earth, both above and beneath: all things bear record of me.[4r]

64. And it came to pass, when the Lord had spoken with Adam, our father, that Adam cried unto the Lord,[4s] and he was caught away by the Spirit of the Lord,[4t] and was carried down into the water, and was laid under the water, and was brought forth out of the water.

65. And thus he was baptized,[4u] and the Spirit of God descended upon him,[4v] and thus he was born of the Spirit,[4w] and became quickened in the inner man.

66. And he heard a voice[4x] out of heaven, saying: Thou art baptized with fire, and with the Holy Ghost.[4y] This is the record of the Father, and the Son,[4z] from henceforth and forever;

67. And thou art after the order of him who was without beginning of days or end of years,[5a] from all eternity to all eternity.

68. Behold, thou art one in me, a son of God; and thus may all become my sons.[5b] Amen.

CHAPTER 7.

THE WRITINGS OF MOSES

As revealed to Joseph Smith the Prophet, in December, 1830—Continued.

1. And it came to pass that Enoch continued his speech, saying: Behold, our father Adam taught these things, and many have believed and become the sons of God,[a] and many have believed not, and have perished in their sins, and are looking forth with fear, in torment, for the fiery indignation of the wrath of God to be poured out upon them.

2. And from that time forth Enoch began to prophesy,[b] saying unto the people, that: As I was journeying, and stood upon the place Mahujah, and cried unto the Lord, there came a voice out of heaven,[c] saying—Turn ye, and get ye upon the mount Simeon.

3. And it came to pass that I turned and went up on the mount; and as I stood upon the mount, I beheld the heavens open, and I was clothed upon with glory;[d]

4. And I saw the Lord;[e] and he stood before my face, and he

4o, compare John 14:16—26. 15:26. 16:7, 13. Moro. 8:26. D. & C. 21:9. 31:11. 42:16, 17. 50:14, 17. 75:10. 88:3, 4. 124:97. 4p, 1:6. 4q, 5:57. 4r, compare D. & C. 88:45—47. 4s, 1:30. 4t, compare 1 Kings 18:12. 2 Kings 2:16. Ezek. 3:12, 14. Acts 8:39. 1 Ne. 11:1. 4u, ver. 52. 4v, compare 1:24. 4w, ver. 59. Compare John 3:5. Mos. 27:24. See also Acts 2:38. Mos. 27:25. Al. 5:14. 22:15. 36:5, 23, 24, 26. 38:6. D. & C. 5:16. 4x, 1:25. 4y, compare Matt. 3:11. Acts 1:5. D. & C. 33:11. 4z, see 1:24. 5a, 1:3. 5b, see 6:8. CHAP. 7: a, see 6:8. b, 5:10. c, see 1:25. d, see 1:2. e, 1:2.

talked with me, even as a man talketh one with another, face to face;[f] and he said unto me: Look,[g] and I will show unto thee the world for the space of many generations.

5. And it came to pass that I beheld in the valley of Shum, and lo, a great people which dwelt in tents, which were the people of Shum.[h]

6. And again the Lord said unto me: Look; and I looked towards the north, and I beheld the people of Canaan,[i] which dwelt in tents.

7. And the Lord said unto me: Prophesy; and I prophesied, saying: Behold the people of Canaan, which are numerous, shall go forth in battle array against the people of Shum, and shall slay them that they shall utterly be destroyed; and the people of Canaan shall divide themselves in the land, and the land shall be barren and unfruitful, and none other people shall dwell there but the people of Canaan;

8. For behold, the Lord shall curse the land with much heat, and the barrenness thereof shall go forth forever; and there was a blackness[j] came upon all the children of Canaan, that they were despised among all people.

9. And it came to pass that the Lord said unto me: Look;[l] and I looked, and I beheld the land of Sharon, and the land of Enoch, and the land of Omner, and the land of Heni, and the land of Shem, and the land of Haner, and the land of Hanannihah, and all the inhabitants thereof;

10. And the Lord said unto me: Go to this people, and say unto them—Repent,[m] lest I come out and smite them with a curse, and they die.

11. And he gave unto me a commandment that I should baptize[n] in the name of the Father, and of the Son,[o] which is full of grace and truth,[p] and of the Holy Ghost,[q] which beareth record[r] of the Father and the Son.

12. And it came to pass that Enoch continued to call upon all the people, save it were the people of Canaan,[s] to repent;[t]

13. And so great was the faith of Enoch, that he led the people of God, and their enemies came to battle against them; and he spake the word of the Lord, and the earth trembled, and the mountains fled, even according to his command; and the rivers of water were turned out of their course;[u] and the roar of the lions was heard out of the wilderness; and all nations feared greatly, so powerful was the word of Enoch, and so great was the power of the language which God had given him.[v]

14. There also came up a land out of the depth of the sea, and so great was the fear of the enemies of the people of God, that they fled and stood afar off and went upon the land which came up out of the depth of the sea.

15. And the giants of the land, also, stood afar off; and there went forth a curse upon all people that fought against God;

16. And from that time forth there were wars and bloodshed among them; but the Lord came and dwelt with his people,[w] and they dwelt in righteousness.[x]

17. The fear of the Lord was upon all nations, so great was

---

f, 1:2.   **g**, 1:4.   **h**, ver. 7.   **i**, compare 6:17.   **j**, ver. 22. Compare 2 Ne. 5:21.   **l**, see 1:4.   **m**, see 5:8.   **n**, see 6:52.   **o**, compare 5:8.   **p**, see 1:6.   **q**, see 1:24.   **r**, see 1:24.   **s**, ver. 8.   **t**, see 5:8.   **u**, 6:34.   **v**, compare 6:32.   **w**, compare ver. 21.   **x**, ver. 18.

the glory of the Lord, which was upon his people. And the Lord blessed the land, and they were blessed upon the mountains, and upon the high places, and did flourish.

18. And the Lord called his people ZION,[y] because they were of one heart and one mind, and dwelt in righteousness; and there was no poor among them.

19. And Enoch continued his preaching in righteousness unto the people of God. And it came to pass in his days, that he built a city that was called the City of Holiness, even ZION.[z]

20. And it came to pass that Enoch talked[2a] with the Lord; and he said unto the Lord: Surely Zion shall dwell in safety forever. But the Lord said unto Enoch: Zion have I blessed, but the residue of the people[2b] have I cursed.

21. And it came to pass that the Lord showed unto Enoch all the inhabitants of the earth;[2c] and he beheld, and lo, Zion, in process of time, was taken up into heaven.[2d] And the Lord said unto Enoch: Behold mine abode forever.

22. And Enoch also beheld the residue of the people which were the sons of Adam; and they were a mixture of all the seed of Adam save it were the seed of Cain, for the seed of Cain were black, and had not place among them.

23. And after that Zion was taken up into heaven, Enoch beheld, and lo, all the nations of the earth were before him;[2e]

24. And there came generation upon generation; and Enoch was high and lifted up, even in the bosom of the Father, and of the Son of Man;[2f] and behold, the power of Satan was upon all the face of the earth.

25. And he saw angels[2g] descending out of heaven; and he heard a loud voice[2h] saying: Wo, wo be unto the inhabitants of the earth.

26. And he beheld Satan;[2i] and he had a great chain in his hand, and it veiled the whole face of the earth with darkness; and he looked up and laughed,[2j] and his angels rejoiced.

27. And Enoch beheld angels descending out of heaven,[2k] bearing testimony of the Father and Son;[2l] and the Holy Ghost[2m] fell on many, and they were caught up by the powers of heaven into Zion.[2n]

28. And it came to pass that the God of heaven looked upon the residue of the people,[2o] and he wept;[2p] and Enoch bore record of it, saying: How is it that the heavens weep, and shed forth their tears as the rain upon the mountains?

29. And Enoch said unto the Lord: How is it that thou canst weep, seeing thou art holy, and from all eternity to all eternity?[2q]

30. And were it possible that man could number the particles of the earth, yea millions of earths like this, it would not be a beginning to the number of thy creations;[2r] and thy curtains are stretched out still; and yet thou art there, and thy bosom is there; and also thou art just; thou art merciful and kind forever;

31. And thou hast taken Zion to thine own bosom,[2s] from all

y, vers. 19—21, 23, 27, 62, 69. Compare D. & C. 38:4. 58:7. 84:99, 100. See also D. & C. 42:35.   z, compare ver. 18.   2a, see 1:30.   2b, ver. 28.   2c, ver. 23.   See also 1:8.   2d, vers. 23, 27, 31, 47, 69. Compare ver. 18. Gen. 5:24. 2e, ver. 21. 1:8.   2f, 6:57.   2g, ver. 27. See also 5:6.   2h, see 1:25. 2i, compare 1:13.   2j, compare 5:21.   2k, ver. 25.   2l, see 1:24.   2m, 1:24. 2n, ver. 21.   2o, ver. 20.   2p, vers. 29, 31, 37, 40.   2q, compare 1:3. 2r, compare 1:28.   2s, ver. 21

thy creations, from all eternity to all eternity; and naught but peace, justice, and truth is the habitation of thy throne; and mercy shall go before thy face and have no end; how is it thou canst weep?[2t]

32. The Lord said[2u] unto Enoch: Behold these thy brethren; they are the workmanship of mine own hands,[2v] and I gave unto them their knowledge, in the day I created them; and in the Garden of Eden,[2w] gave I unto man his agency;[2x]

33. And unto thy brethren have I said, and also given commandment, that they should love one another, and that they should choose me, their Father;[2y] but behold, they are without affection, and they hate their own blood;[2z]

34. And the fire of mine indignation is kindled against them; and in my hot displeasure will I send in the floods[3a] upon them, for my fierce anger is kindled against them.[3b]

35. Behold, I am God; Man of Holiness[3c] is my name; Man of Counsel is my name; and Endless[3d] and Eternal is my name, also.

36. Wherefore, I can stretch forth mine hands and hold all the creations which I have made; and mine eye can pierce them also, and among all the workmanship of mine hands[3e] there has not been so great wickedness as among thy brethren.

37. But behold, their sins shall be upon the heads of their fathers; Satan shall be their father, and misery shall be their doom;[3f]

and the whole heavens shall weep over them, even all the workmanship of mine hands; wherefore should not the heavens weep,[3g] seeing these shall suffer?

38. But behold, these which thine eyes are upon shall perish in the floods;[3h] and behold, I will shut them up; a prison have I prepared for them.[3i]

39. And That which I have chosen hath plead before my face. Wherefore, he suffereth for their sins;[3j] inasmuch as they will repent in the day that my Chosen[3k] shall return unto me, and until that day they shall be in torment;

40. Wherefore, for this shall the heavens weep,[3l] yea, and all the workmanship of mine hands.[3m]

41. And it came to pass that the Lord spake unto Enoch,[3n] and told Enoch all the doings of the children of men; wherefore Enoch knew, and looked upon their wickedness, and their misery, and wept and stretched forth his arms, and his heart swelled wide as eternity; and his bowels yearned; and all eternity shook.

42. And Enoch also saw Noah,[3o] and his family; that the posterity of all the sons of Noah should be saved with a temporal salvation;

43. Wherefore Enoch saw that Noah built an ark;[3p] and that the Lord smiled upon it, and held it in his own hand; but upon the residue of the wicked the floods[3q] came and swallowed them up.

44. And as Enoch saw this, he had bitterness of soul, and wept[3r] over his brethren, and said unto the heavens: I will refuse to be comforted; but the Lord said[3s]

2t, ver. 28.   2u, 1:1.   2v, see 1:4.   2w, 3:8.   2x, 3:17.   2y, 6:33.
2z, 6:15.   3a, vers. 38, 43, 51.   8:17, 24.   Compare Gen. 6:17.   7:4, 10.   3b, 6:27.
3c, 6:57.   Compare 1:3.   3d, 1:3.   3e, 1:4.   3f, compare 6:29.   3g, ver. 28.
3h, ver. 34.   3i, compare ver. 57.   1 Pet. 3:18—20.   3j, compare 1:6.   5:9.
3k, 4:2.   3l, ver. 28.   3m, ver. 36.   3n, 1:1.   3o, vers. 45, 50.   8:8—30.
3p, compare Gen. chaps. 6, 7, 8.   See also Eth. 2:6.   6:4—11.   3q, ver. 34.
3r, vers. 49, 58.   3s, 1:1.

unto Enoch: Lift up your heart, and be glad; and look.[3t]

45. And it came to pass that Enoch looked; and from Noah, he beheld all the families of the earth; and he cried unto the Lord, saying: When shall the day of the Lord come? When shall the blood of the Righteous be shed, that all they that mourn may be sanctified and have eternal life?[3u]

46. And the Lord said: It shall be in the meridian of time,[3v] in the days of wickedness and vengeance.

47. And behold, Enoch saw the day of the coming of the Son of Man,[3w] even in the flesh;[3x] and his soul rejoiced, saying: The Righteous is lifted up, and the Lamb is slain from the foundation of the world; and through faith I am in the bosom of the Father, and behold, Zion is with me.[3y]

48. And it came to pass that Enoch looked upon the earth; and he heard a voice[3z] from the bowels thereof, saying: Wo, wo is me,[4a] the mother of men; I am pained, I am weary, because of the wickedness of my children. When shall I rest,[4b] and be cleansed from the filthiness which is gone forth out of me? When will my Creator sanctify me, that I may rest, and righteousness for a season abide upon my face?

49. And when Enoch heard the earth mourn, he wept,[4c] and cried unto the Lord, saying: O Lord, wilt thou not have compassion upon the earth? Wilt thou not bless the children of Noah?

50. And it came to pass that Enoch continued his cry unto the Lord, saying: I ask thee, O Lord, in the name of thine Only Begotten,[4d] even Jesus Christ,[4e] that thou wilt have mercy upon Noah and his seed, that the earth might never more be covered by the floods.

51. And the Lord could not withhold; and he covenanted with Enoch, and sware unto him with an oath, that he would stay the floods; that he would call upon the children of Noah;

52. And he sent forth an unalterable decree, that a remnant of his seed should always be found among all nations, while the earth should stand;

53. And the Lord said: Blessed is he through whose seed Messiah shall come; for he saith—I am Messiah, the King of Zion, the Rock of Heaven, which is broad as eternity; whoso cometh in at the gate and climbeth up by me shall never fall; wherefore, blessed are they of whom I have spoken, for they shall come forth with songs of everlasting joy.

54. And it came to pass that Enoch cried unto the Lord,[4f] saying: When the Son of Man[4g] cometh in the flesh,[4h] shall the earth rest?[4i] I pray thee, show me these things.

55. And the Lord said unto Enoch: Look,[4j] and he looked and beheld the Son of Man lifted up on the cross,[4k] after the manner of men;

56. And he heard a loud voice;[4l] and the heavens were veiled; and all the creations of God mourned; and the earth groaned;[4m] and the rocks were rent; and the saints arose, and

3t, 1:4.   3u, compare ver. 39.   3v, 5:57.   3w, 5:57.   3x, ver. 54. 3y, compare ver. 21.   3z, compare 1:25.   4a, compare ver. 56.   4b, vers. 54, 58, 61, 64.   4c, ver. 44.   4d, 1:6.   4e, 6:52.   4f, 1:30.   4g, 6:57.   4h, ver. 47.   4i, ver. 48.   4j, 1:4.   4k, compare ver. 47. 1 Ne. 11:33.   3 Ne. 27:14. Eth. 4:1. See also Matt. 27:35. Mark 15:24. Luke 23:33. John 19:18.   4l, 1:25. 4m, compare ver. 48.

were crowned at the right hand of the Son of Man,[4n] with crowns of glory;

57. And as many of the spirits as were in prison[4o] came forth, and stood on the right hand of God; and the remainder were reserved in chains of darkness until the judgment of the great day.

58. And again Enoch wept[4p] and cried unto the Lord, saying: When shall the earth rest?[4q]

59. And Enoch beheld the Son of Man ascend up unto the Father; and he called unto the Lord, saying: Wilt thou not come again upon the earth? Forasmuch as thou art God, and I know thee, and thou hast sworn unto me,[4r] and commanded me that I should ask in the name of thine Only Begotten;[4s] thou hast made me, and given unto me a right to thy throne, and not of myself, but through thine own grace; wherefore, I ask thee if thou wilt not come again on the earth.

60. And the Lord said[4t] unto Enoch: As I live, even so will I come in the last days, in the days of wickedness and vengeance, to fulfil the oath which I have made unto you[4u] concerning the children of Noah;

61. And the day shall come that the earth shall rest, but before that day the heavens shall be darkened, and a veil of darkness shall cover the earth; and the heavens shall shake, and also the earth; and great tribulations shall be among the children of men, but my people will I preserve;

62. And righteousness will I send down out of heaven; and truth will I send forth out of the earth,[4v] to bear testimony of mine Only Begotten;[4w] his resurrection from the dead; yea, and also the resurrection of all men; and righteousness and truth will I cause to sweep the earth as with a flood, to gather out mine elect from the four quarters of the earth, unto a place which I shall prepare, an Holy City, that my people may gird up their loins, and be looking forth for the time of my coming; for there shall be my tabernacle, and it shall be called Zion,[4x] a New Jerusalem.[4y]

63. And the Lord said unto Enoch: Then shalt thou and all thy city[4z] meet them there, and we will receive them into our bosom, and they shall see us; and we will fall upon their necks, and they shall fall upon our necks, and we will kiss each other;

64. And there shall be mine abode,[5a] and it shall be Zion, which shall come forth out of all the creations which I have made; and for the space of a thousand years[5b] the earth shall rest.[5c]

65. And it came to pass that Enoch saw the day of the coming of the Son of Man,[5d] in the last days, to dwell on the earth in righteousness for the space of a thousand years;[5e]

66. But before that day he saw great tribulations among the wicked; and he also saw the sea, that it was troubled, and men's hearts failing them, looking forth with fear for the judgments of the Almighty God, which should come upon the wicked.

67. And the Lord showed

4n, ver. 54.   4o, compare ver. 38.   Isa. 42:7.   49:9.   61:1.   1 Pet. 3:18—20.
D. & C. 76:73.   88:99.   4p, ver. 44.   4q, ver. 48.   4r, ver. 51.   4s, ver. 50.
4t, 1:1.   4u, ver. 51.   4v, compare Ps. 85:11.   Isa. 45:8.   4w, see 1:6.
4x, compare ver. 19.   4y, compare Gal. 4:26.   Heb. 12:22.   Rev. 3:12.   21:2, 10.
Eth. 13:3—8.   D. & C. 42:9, 35, 67.   45:66.   84:2, 3, 4.   4z, compare D. & C.
45:12.   78:4.   5a, compare ver. 21.   5b, ver. 65.   Compare Rev. 20:2—7.   D. & C. 29:11, 22.   43:30.   84:119.   88:101, 108—110.   5c, ver. 48.   5d, ver. 54.
5e, ver. 64.

Enoch all things, even unto the end of the world; and he saw the day of the righteous, the hour of their redemption; and received a fulness of joy;

68. And all the days of Zion,[5f] in the days of Enoch, were three hundred and sixty-five years.

69. And Enoch and all his people walked with God,[5g] and he dwelt in the midst of Zion; and it came to pass that Zion was not, for God received it up into his own bosom; and from thence went forth the saying, ZION IS FLED.[5h]

CHAPTER 8.

THE WRITINGS OF MOSES

As revealed to Joseph Smith the Prophet, in December, 1830—Concluded.

1. And all the days of Enoch were four hundred and thirty years.

2. And it came to pass that Methuselah,[a] the son of Enoch, was not taken, that the covenants of the Lord might be fulfilled, which he made to Enoch;[b] for he truly covenanted with Enoch that Noah should be of the fruit of his loins.

3. And it came to pass that Methuselah prophesied[c] that from his loins should spring all the kingdoms of the earth (through Noah), and he took glory unto himself.

4. And there came forth a great famine into the land, and the Lord cursed the earth with a sore curse, and many of the inhabitants thereof died.

5.[d] And it came to pass that Methuselah lived one hundred and eighty-seven years, and begat Lamech;

6. And Methuselah lived, after he begat Lamech, seven hundred and eighty-two years, and begat sons and daughters;

7. And all the days of Methuselah were nine hundred and sixty-nine years, and he died.

8. And Lamech lived one hundred and eighty-two years, and begat a son,

9. And he called his name Noah,[e] saying: This son shall comfort us concerning our work and toil of our hands, because of the ground which the Lord hath cursed.[f]

10. And Lamech lived, after he begat Noah, five hundred and ninety-five years, and begat sons and daughters;

11. And all the days of Lamech were seven hundred and seventy-seven years, and he died.

12. And Noah was four hundred and fifty years old, and begat Japheth; and forty-two years afterward he begat Shem of her who was the mother of Japheth, and when he was five hundred years old he begat Ham.[g]

13. And Noah and his sons hearkened[h] unto the Lord, and gave heed, and they were called the sons of God.[i]

14.[j] And when these men began to multiply on the face of the earth, and daughters were born unto them, the sons of men[k] saw that those daughters were fair, and they took them wives, even as they chose.

15. And the Lord said[l] unto Noah: The daughters of thy sons have sold themselves; for behold mine anger is kindled[m] against the sons of men,[n] for they will not hearken[o] to my voice.

16. And it came to pass that

5f, ver. 21. **5g,** 6:34. **5h,** ver. 21. Compare Gen. 5:24.
CHAP. 8: **a,** 6:25. **b,** 7:51. **c,** compare 5:10. **d,** compare vers. 5—12 with Gen. 5:25—32, verse by verse. **e,** 7:42. **f,** 4:23. 5:37. **g,** Abraham, 1:11, 21—27. **h,** 5:17. **i,** 6:7. **j,** compare Gen. 6:1, 2. **k,** 5:52. **l,** 1:3. **m,** 6:27. **n,** 5:52. **o,** 4:4. Compare 5:16.

Noah prophesied,[p] and taught the things of God, even as it was in the beginning.

17.[q] And the Lord said[r] unto Noah: My Spirit[s] shall not always strive with man,[t] for he shall know that all flesh shall die; yet his days shall be an hundred and twenty years; and if men do not repent,[u] I will send in the floods[v] upon them.

18. And in those days there were giants on the earth,[w] and they sought Noah to take away his life; but the Lord was with Noah, and the power of the Lord[x] was upon him.

19. And the Lord ordained[y] Noah after his own order, and commanded him that he should go forth and declare his Gospel[z] unto the children of men, even as it was given unto Enoch.[2a]

20. And it came to pass that Noah called upon the children of men[2b] that they should repent;[2c] but they hearkened not[2d] unto his words;

21. And also, after that they had heard him, they came up before him, saying: Behold, we are the sons of God;[2e] have we not taken unto ourselves the daughters of men? And are we not eating and drinking, and marrying and giving in marriage? And our wives bear unto us children, and the same are mighty men, which are like unto men of old, men of great renown.[2f] And they hearkened not[2g] unto the words of Noah.

22. And God saw that the wickedness of men had become great in the earth; and every man was lifted up in the imagination of the thoughts of his heart, being only evil continually.[2h]

23. And it came to pass that Noah continued his preaching unto the people, saying: Hearken, and give heed unto my words;

24. Believe and repent[2i] of your sins and be baptized[2j] in the name of Jesus Christ,[2k] the Son of God,[2l] even as our fathers, and ye shall receive the Holy Ghost,[2m] that ye may have all things made manifest; and if ye do not this, the floods[2n] will come in upon you; nevertheless they hearkened not.[2o]

25. And it repented Noah,[2p] and his heart was pained that the Lord had made man on the earth, and it grieved him at the heart.

26. And the Lord said: I will destroy man[2q] whom I have created, from the face of the earth, both man and beast, and the creeping things, and the fowls of the air; for it repenteth Noah that I have created them, and that I have made them; and he hath called upon me; for they have sought his life.[2r]

27. And thus Noah found grace in the eyes of the Lord;[2s] for Noah was a just man, and perfect in his generation; and he walked with God,[2t] as did also his three sons,[2u] Shem, Ham, and Japheth.[2v]

28. The earth was corrupt before God, and it was filled with violence.

29. And God looked upon the

---

p, 5:10. **q,** compare Gen. 6:3. **r,** ver. 15. **s,** 1:15. 6:34. **t,** Gen. 6:3. Compare 2 Ne. 26:11. Eth. 2:15. D. & C. 1:33. **u,** compare 5:8. **v,** 7:34. **w,** compare Gen. 6:4. **x,** Abraham 1:18. **y,** compare 6:7. **z,** 5:58. **2a,** 6:27, 32. **2b,** 5:52. **2c,** 5:8. **2d,** 5:16. Compare 4:4. **2e,** see 6:7. **2f,** compare Gen. 6:4. **2g,** ver. 20. **2h,** compare Gen. 6:5. **2i,** 5:8. **2j,** 6:52. **2k,** 6:52. **2l,** 1:6. **2m,** 1:24. **2n,** see 7:34. **2o,** ver. 20. **2p,** see ver. 26. Compare Gen. 6:6. **2q,** ver. 30. Compare Gen. 6:7. **2r,** ver. 18. **2s,** compare Gen. 6:8, 9. **2t,** 6:34. **2u,** ver. 12. **2v,** compare vers. 28—30 with Gen. 6:11—13.

earth, and, behold, it was corrupt, for all flesh had corrupted its way upon the earth.

30. And God said unto Noah: The end of all flesh is come before me, for the earth is filled with violence, and behold I will destroy all flesh from off the earth.[2w]

2w, ver. 26.

No. 1.

EXPLANATION OF THE ABOVE CUT.

Fig. 1. The Angel of the Lord. 2. Abraham fastened upon an altar. 3. The idolatrous priest of Elkenah attempting to offer up Abraham as a sacrifice. 4. The altar for sacrifice by the idolatrous priests, standing before the gods of Elkenah, Libnah, Mahmackrah, Korash, and Pharaoh. 5. The idolatrous god of Elkenah. 6. The idolatrous god of Libnah. 7. The idolatrous god of Mahmackrah. 8. The idolatrous god of Korash. 9. The idolatrous god of Pharaoh. 10. Abraham in Egypt. 11. Designed to represent the pillars of heaven, as understood by the Egyptians. 12. Raukeeyang, signifying expanse, or the firmament over our heads; but in this case, in relation to this subject, the Egyptians meant it to signify Shaumau, to be high, or the heavens, answering to the Hebrew word, Shaumahyeem.

THE BOOK OF ABRAHAM

TRANSLATED FROM THE PAPYRUS, BY JOSEPH SMITH.

A Translation of some ancient Records, that have fallen into our hands from the catacombs of Egypt. —— The writings of Abraham while he was in Egypt, called the Book of Abraham, written by his own hand, upon papyrus. See History of the Church, vol. 2, pp. 235, 236, 348-351.

CHAPTER 1.

1. In the land of the Chaldeans,[a] at the residence of my father, I, Abraham, saw that it was needful for me to obtain another place of residence;

2. And, finding there was greater happiness and peace and rest for me, I sought for the blessings of the fathers,[b] and the right whereunto I should be ordained[c] to administer the same; having been myself a follower of righteousness, desiring also to be one who possessed great knowledge, and to be a greater follower of righteousness, and to possess a greater knowledge, and to be a father of many nations,[d] a prince of peace, and desiring to receive instructions, and to keep the commandments of God, I became a rightful heir, a High Priest, holding the right belonging to the fathers.[e]

3. It was conferred upon me from the fathers; it came down from the fathers,[f] from the beginning of time, yea, even from the beginning, or before the foundations of the earth to the present time, even the right of the firstborn, on the first man,[g] who is Adam,[h] our first father, through the fathers, unto me.

4. I sought for mine appointment unto the Priesthood[i] according to the appointment of God unto the fathers concerning the seed.[j]

5. My fathers having turned from their righteousness, and from the holy commandments which the Lord their God had given unto them, unto the worshiping of the gods of the heathen,[k] utterly refused to hearken to my voice;

6. For their hearts were set to do evil, and were wholly turned to the god of Elkenah,[l] and the god of Libnah, and the god of Mahmackrah, and the god of Korash, and the god of Pharaoh,[m] king of Egypt;

7. Therefore they turned their hearts to the sacrifice of the heathen in offering up their children unto their dumb idols, and hearkened not unto my voice, but endeavored to take away my life[n] by the hand of the priest of Elkenah. The priest of Elkenah was also the priest of Pharaoh.[o]

8. Now, at this time it was the custom of the priest of Pharaoh, the king of Egypt, to offer up upon the altar which was built in the land of Chaldea, for the offering unto these strange gods, men, women, and children.

9. And it came to pass that the

---

a, vers. 20, 29, 30.   Gen. 11:28.   **b,** vers. 3, 4.   **c,** compare Moses 8:19. **d,** compare Gen. 12:2. 17:6. 18:18.   **e,** vers. 3, 4.   **f,** compare D. & C. 84:6—17.   **g,** Moses 3:7.   **h,** Moses 1:34.   **i,** Moses 6:7. D. & C. 84:14. **j,** compare D. & C. 84:6—17.   **k,** ver. 7.   **l,** vers. 7, 13, 17, 29.   **m,** ver. 9. **n,** vers. 12, 15, 17, 30.   **o,** vers. 8, 10.

priest made an offering unto the god of Pharaoh,[p] and also unto the god of Shagreel, even after the manner of the Egyptians. Now the god of Shagreel was the sun.

10. Even the thank-offering of a child did the priest of Pharaoh offer upon the altar which stood by the hill called Potiphar's Hill,[q] at the head of the plain of Olishem.

11. Now, this priest had offered upon this altar three virgins[r] at one time, who were the daughters of Onitah, one of the royal descent directly from the loins of Ham.[s] These virgins were offered up because of their virtue; they would not bow down to worship gods of wood or of stone, therefore they were killed upon this altar, and it was done after the manner of the Egyptians.

12. And it came to pass that the priests laid violence upon me, that they might slay me also,[t] as they did those virgins[u] upon this altar; and that you may have a knowledge of this altar, I will refer you to the representation at the commencement of this record.

13. It was made after the form of a bedstead, such as was had among the Chaldeans,[v] and it stood before the gods of Elkenah, Libnah, Mahmackrah, Korash, and also a god like unto that of Pharaoh, king of Egypt.[w]

14. That you may have an understanding of these gods, I have given you the fashion of them in the figures at the beginning, which manner of the figures is called by the Chaldeans Rah-leenos, which signifies hieroglyphics.

15. And as they lifted up their hands upon me, that they might offer me up and take away my life,[x] behold, I lifted up my voice unto the Lord my God,[y] and the Lord hearkened and heard, and he filled me with the vision of the Almighty, and the angel of his presence stood by me,[z] and immediately unloosed my bands;

16. And his voice was unto me: Abraham, Abraham, behold, my name is Jehovah,[2a] and I have heard thee, and have come down to deliver thee, and to take thee away from thy father's house, and from all thy kins-folk, into a strange land which thou knowest not of;[2b]

17. And this because they have turned their hearts away from me, to worship the god[2c] of Elkenah, and the god of Libnah, and the god of Mahmackrah, and the god of Korash, and the god of Pharaoh, king of Egypt; therefore I have come down to visit them, and to destroy him who hath lifted up his hand against thee, Abraham, my son, to take away thy life.[2d]

18. Behold, I will lead thee by my hand, and I will take thee, to put upon thee my name, even the Priesthood[2e] of thy father, and my power shall be over thee.[2f]

19. As it was with Noah[2g] so shall it be with thee; but through thy ministry my name shall be known in the earth forever, for I am thy God.

20. Behold, Potiphar's Hill[2h] was in the land of Ur, of Chaldea.[2i] And the Lord broke down

---

p, ver. 6.   q, ver. 20.   r, ver. 12.   s, Moses 8:12.   t, ver. 7.   u, ver. 11.   v, ver. 1.   w, ver. 6.   x, see ver. 7.   y, Moses 1:30.   z, 2:13. 3:20. 2a, 2:8. Compare Moses 1:3. 7:35.   2b, 2:3, 6.   2c, ver. 6.   2d, ver. 7. 2e, Moses 6:7.   2f, Moses 8:18.   2g, Moses 8:19—27.   2h, ver. 10.   2i, ver. 1. 2:1. 2:15. 3:1. See also Gen. 11:28, 31.

the altar of Elkenah,[2j] and of the gods of the land, and utterly destroyed them, and smote the priest that he died; and there was great mourning in Chaldea, and also in the court of Pharaoh; which Pharaoh signifies king by royal blood.

21. Now this king of Egypt was a descendant from the loins of Ham,[2k] and was a partaker of the blood of the Canaanites by birth.

22. From this descent sprang all the Egyptians, and thus the blood of the Canaanites was preserved in the land.

23. The land of Egypt being first discovered by a woman, who was the daughter of Ham, and the daughter of Egyptus, which in the Chaldean signifies Egypt, which signifies that which is forbidden.

24. When this woman discovered the land it was under water, who afterward settled her sons in it; and thus, from Ham,[2l] sprang that race which preserved the curse in the land.[2m]

25. Now the first government of Egypt was established by Pharaoh,[2n] the eldest son of Egyptus, the daughter of Ham, and it was after the manner of the government of Ham, which was patriarchal.[2o]

26. Pharaoh, being a righteous man, established his kingdom and judged his people wisely and justly all his days, seeking earnestly to imitate that order established by the fathers in the first generations, in the days of the first patriarchal reign, even in the reign of Adam, and also of Noah, his father, who blessed him with the blessings of the earth, and with the blessings of wisdom, but cursed him as pertaining to the Priesthood.

27. Now, Pharaoh[2p] being of that lineage by which he could not have the right of Priesthood, notwithstanding the Pharaohs would fain claim it from Noah, through Ham,[2q] therefore my father was led away by their idolatry;[2r]

28. But I shall endeavor, hereafter, to delineate the chronology running back from myself to the beginning of the creation, for the records[2s] have come into my hands, which I hold unto this present time.

29. Now, after the priest of Elkenah was smitten that he died,[2t] there came a fulfilment of those things which were said unto me concerning the land of Chaldea,[2u] that there should be a famine in the land.[2v]

30. Accordingly a famine prevailed throughout all the land of Chaldea, and my father was sorely tormented because of the famine, and he repented of the evil which he had determined against me, to take away my life.[2w]

31. But the records of the fathers,[2x] even the patriarchs, concerning the right of Priesthood,[2y] the Lord my God preserved in mine own hands; therefore a knowledge of the beginning of the creation, and also of the planets, and of the stars,[2z] as they were made known unto the fathers, have I kept even unto this day, and I shall endeavor to write some of these things upon this record, for the benefit of my posterity that shall come after me.

2j, ver. 6.   2k, Moses 8:12.   2l, ver. 21.   2m, compare ver. 26.   2n, vers. 26, 27.   2o, ver. 26.   2p, ver. 25.   2q, Moses 8:12.   2r, ver. 5.   2s, compare Moses 6:5.   2t, ver. 20.   2u, ver. 20.   2v, ver. 30. 2:1, 17.   2w, ver. 7. 2x, compare ver. 28.   Moses 6:5.   2y, Moses 6:7.   2z, compare chap. 3.

CHAPTER 2.

1. Now the Lord God caused the famine[a] to wax sore in the land of Ur, insomuch that Haran, my brother, died; but Terah, my father, yet lived in the land of Ur, of the Chaldees.[b]

2. And it came to pass that I, Abraham, took Sarai to wife, and Nehor, my brother, took Milcah to wife, who were the daughters of Haran.[c]

3. Now the Lord had said unto me: Abraham, get thee out of thy country, and from thy kindred, and from thy father's house, unto a land that I will show thee.[d]

4. Therefore I left the land of Ur, of the Chaldees,[e] to go into the land of Canaan;[f] and I took Lot, my brother's son, and his wife, and Sarai my wife; and also my father[g] followed after me, unto the land which we denominated Haran.[h]

5. And the famine abated; and my father tarried in Haran and dwelt there, as there were many flocks in Haran; and my father turned again unto his idolatry,[i] therefore he continued in Haran.

6. But I, Abraham, and Lot, my brother's son, prayed unto the Lord, and the Lord appeared unto me, and said unto me:[j] Arise, and take Lot with thee; for I have purposed to take thee away out of Haran,[k] and to make of thee a minister to bear my name in a strange land which I will give unto thy seed after thee for an everlasting possession, when they hearken to my voice.

7. For I am the Lord thy God; I dwell in heaven; the earth is my footstool;[l] I stretch my hand over the sea, and it obeys my voice; I cause the wind and the fire to be my chariot; I say to the mountains—Depart hence—and behold, they are taken away by a whirlwind, in an instant, suddenly.

8. My name is Jehovah,[m] and I know the end from the beginning;[n] therefore my hand shall be over thee.

9. And I will make of thee a great nation,[o] and I will bless thee above measure,[p] and make thy name great among all nations, and thou shalt be a blessing unto thy seed after thee,[q] that in their hands they shall bear this ministry and Priesthood[r] unto all nations;

10. And I will bless them through thy name; for as many as receive this Gospel[s] shall be called after thy name, and shall be accounted thy seed, and shall rise up and bless thee, as their father;

11. And I will bless them that bless thee, and curse them that curse thee; and in thee (that is, in thy Priesthood) and in thy seed (that is, thy Priesthood), for I give unto thee a promise that this right shall continue in thee, and in thy seed after thee (that is to say, the literal seed, or the seed of the body) shall all the families of the earth be blessed,[t] even with the blessings of the Gospel,[u] which are the blessings of salvation,[v] even of life eternal.

12. Now, after the Lord had withdrawn[w] from speaking to me,

a, 1:29.   **b,** 1:20. Gen. 11:28.   **c,** Gen. 11:29.   **d,** compare 1:16, and Gen. 12:1.   **e,** ver. 1.   **f,** compare Moses 6:41.   **g,** ver. 1.   **h,** compare ver. 1.   See also Gen. 11:31.   12:4.   **i,** 1:5.   **j,** Moses 1:1.   **k,** ver. 4. **l,** Moses 6:9.   **m,** 1:16.   **n,** compare Moses 1:3.   **o,** 1:2.   3:14.   Compare Gen. 12:2.   **p,** compare Gen. 12:1—3.   15:18. 1 Ne. 15:18.   17:40.   22:9.   2 Ne. 29:14.   3 Ne. 20:27.   Morm. 5:20.   **q,** compare Gen. 12:2.   **r,** Moses 6:7. **s,** Moses 5:58.   **t,** compare Gen. 12:3.   18:18.   22:18.   26:4.   **u,** Moses 5:58. **v,** Moses 6:59.   **w,** Moses 1:9.

and withdrawn his face from me, I said in my heart: Thy servant has sought thee earnestly; now I have found thee;

13. Thou didst send thine angel*x* to deliver me from the gods of Elkenah, and I will do well to hearken unto thy voice, therefore let thy servant rise up and depart in peace.

14. So I, Abraham, departed as the Lord had said unto me, and Lot with me;*y* and I, Abraham, was sixty and two years old when I departed out of Haran.*z*

15. And I took Sarai, whom I took to wife when I was in Ur, in Chaldea,*2a* and Lot, my brother's son, and all our substance that we had gathered, and the souls that we had won in Haran, and came forth in the way to the land of Canaan,*2b* and dwelt in tents as we came on our way;

16. Therefore, eternity was our covering and our rock and our salvation, as we journeyed from Haran by the way of Jershon, to come to the land of Canaan.*2c*

17. Now I, Abraham, built an altar in the land of Jershon, and made an offering unto the Lord, and prayed that the famine*2d* might be turned away from my father's house, that they might not perish.

18. And then we passed from Jershon through the land unto the place of Sechem; it was situated in the plains of Moreh, and we had already come into the borders of the land of the Canaanites,*2e* and I offered sacrifice there in the plains of Moreh, and called on the Lord devoutly, because we had already come into the land of this idolatrous nation.

19. And the Lord appeared unto me in answer to my prayers, and said unto me: Unto thy seed will I give this land.*2f*

20. And I, Abraham, arose from the place of the altar which I had built unto the Lord, and removed from thence unto a mountain on the east of Bethel, and pitched my tent there, Bethel on the west, and Hai on the east; and there I built another altar unto the Lord, and called again upon the name of the Lord.*2g*

21.*2h* And I, Abraham, journeyed, going on still towards the south; and there was a continuation of a famine in the land; and I, Abraham, concluded to go down into Egypt, to sojourn there, for the famine became very grievous.

22. And it came to pass when I was come near to enter into Egypt, the Lord said unto me: Behold, Sarai, thy wife, is a very fair woman to look upon;

23. Therefore it shall come to pass, when the Egyptians shall see her, they will say—She is his wife; and they will kill you, but they will save her alive; therefore see that ye do on this wise:

24. Let her say unto the Egyptians, she is thy sister, and thy soul shall live.

25. And it came to pass that I, Abraham, told Sarai, my wife, all that the Lord had said unto me— Therefore say unto them, I pray thee, thou art my sister, that it may be well with me for thy sake, and my soul shall live because of thee.

CHAPTER 3.

1. And I, Abraham, had the Urim and Thummim,*a* which the

---

x, 1:16.   y, ver. 6.   z, ver. 4.   2a, ver. 1.   2b, ver. 4.   2c, compare Gen. 12 و.   2d, 1:29.   2e, 1:21, 22. Compare Gen. 12:6.   2f, ver. 6. Compare Gen. 12:7. 13:15. 17:8.   2g, Gen. 12:8.   2h, compare vers. 21—25. with Gen. 12:9—13.   CHAP. 3: a, ver. 4. Compare Joseph Smith 2:35, 59, 62. Ex. 28:30. Lev. 8:8. Deut. 33:8. Ezra. 2:63. Neh. 7:65. Om. 20—22. Mos. 8:13, 19. 21:27, 28. 28:13—16. Al. 37:23—26. Eth. 3:23, 28.   4:5. D. & C. 10:1. 17:1. 130:9.

A FACSIMILE FROM THE BOOK OF ABRAHAM

No. 2.

EXPLANATION OF THE FOREGOING CUT

Fig. 1.   Kolob, signifying the first creation, nearest to the celestial, or the residence of God.   First in government, the last pertaining to the measurement of time.   The measurement according to celestial time, which celestial time signifies one day to a cubit.   One day in Kolob is equal to a thousand years according to the measurement of this earth, which is called by the Egyptians Jah-oh-eh.

Fig. 2.   Stands next to Kolob, called by the Egyptians Oliblish, which is the next grand governing creation near to the celestial or the place where God resides; holding the key of power also, pertaining to other planets; as revealed from God to Abraham, as he offered sacrifice upon an altar, which he had built unto the Lord.

Fig. 3.   Is made to represent God, sitting upon his throne, clothed with power and authority; with a crown of eternal light upon his head; representing also the grand Key-words of the Holy Priesthood, as revealed to Adam in the Garden of Eden, as also to Seth, Noah, Melchizedek, Abraham, and all to whom the Priesthood was revealed.

Fig. 4.   Answers to the Hebrew word Raukeeyang, signifying expanse, or the firmament of the heavens; also a numerical figure, in Egyptian signifying one thousand; answering to the measuring of the time of Oliblish, which is equal with Kolob in its revolution and in its measuring of time.

Fig. 5.   Is called in Egyptian Enish-go-on-dosh; this is one of the governing planets also, and is said by the Egyptians to be the Sun, and to borrow its light from Kolob through the medium of Kae-e-vanrash, which is the grand Key, or, in other words, the governing power, which governs fifteen other fixed planets or stars, as also Floeese or the Moon, the Earth and the Sun in their annual revolutions.   This planet receives its power through the medium of Kli-flos-is-es, or Hah-ko-kau-beam, the stars represented by numbers 22 and 23, receiving light from the revolutions of Kolob.

Fig. 6.   Represents this earth in its four quarters.

Fig. 7.   Represents God sitting upon his throne, revealing through the heavens the grand Key-words of the Priesthood; as, also, the sign of the Holy Ghost unto Abraham, in the form of a dove.

Fig. 8.   Contains writing that cannot be revealed unto the world; but is to be had in the Holy Temple of God.

Fig. 9.   Ought not to be revealed at the present time.

Fig. 10.   Also.

Fig. 11.   Also.   If the world can find out these numbers, so let it be.   Amen.

Figures 12, 13, 14, 15, 16, 17, 18, 19, and 20, will be given in the own due time of the Lord.

The above translation is given as far as we have any right to give at the present time.

Lord my God had given unto me, in Ur of the Chaldees;[b]

2. And I saw the stars, that they were very great, and that one of them was nearest unto the throne of God; and there were many great ones which were near unto it;

3. And the Lord said unto me: These are the governing ones; and the name of the great one is Kolob,[c] because it is near unto me, for I am the Lord thy God: I have set this one to govern all those which belong to the same order as that upon which thou standest.[d]

4. And the Lord said unto me, by the Urim and Thummim,[e] that Kolob[f] was after the manner of the Lord, according to its times and seasons in the revolutions thereof; that one revolution was a day unto the Lord, after his manner of reckoning,[g] it being one thousand years[h] according to the time appointed unto that whereon thou standest. This is the reckoning of the Lord's time, according to the reckoning of Kolob.[i]

5. And the Lord said unto me: The planet which is the lesser light, lesser than that which is to rule the day, even the night, is above or greater than that upon which thou standest in point of reckoning, for it moveth in order more slow; this is in order because it standeth above the earth upon which thou standest, therefore the reckoning of its time is not so many as to its number of days, and of months, and of years.

6. And the Lord said unto me: Now, Abraham, these two facts exist,[j] behold thine eyes see it;

it is given unto thee to know the times of reckoning, and the set time, yea, the set time of the earth upon which thou standest, and the set time of the greater light which is set to rule the day, and the set time of the lesser light which is set to rule the night.[k]

7. Now the set time of the lesser light is a longer time as to its reckoning than the reckoning of the time of the earth upon which thou standest.

8. And where these two facts exist,[l] there shall be another fact above them, that is, there shall be another planet whose reckoning of time shall be longer still;

9. And thus there shall be the reckoning of the time of one planet above another, until thou come nigh unto Kolob,[m] which Kolob is after the reckoning of the Lord's time;[n] which Kolob is set nigh unto the throne of God, to govern all those planets which belong to the same order as that upon which thou standest.

10. And it is given unto thee to know the set time of all the stars that are set to give light, until thou come near unto the throne of God.[o]

11. Thus I, Abraham, talked with the Lord,[p] face to face,[q] as one man talketh with another; and he told me of the works which his hands had made;[r]

12. And he said unto me: My son, my son (and his hand was stretched out), behold I will show you all these. And he put his hand upon mine eyes, and I saw those things which his hands had made, which were many; and they multiplied before mine eyes,

---

b, 1:20.   c, vers. 9, 16.   5:13.   d, ver. 7.   e, ver. 1.   f, ver. 3.
g, compare vers. 7—9.   5:13.   h, compare Ps. 90:4.   2 Pet. 3:8.   i, ver. 3.
j, vers. 8, 16, 19.   k, compare Moses 2:18.   l, ver. 6.   m, ver. 3.   n, ver. 4.
o, compare ver. 3.   p, Moses 1:2.   q, Moses 1:2.   r, ver. 21.   Compare
Moses 1:4.

and I could not see the end thereof.[s]

13. And he said unto me: This is Shinehah, which is the sun. And he said unto me: Kokob, which is star. And he said unto me: Olea, which is the moon. And he said unto me: Kokaubeam,[t] which signifies stars, or all the great lights, which were in the firmament of heaven.

14. And it was in the night time when the Lord spake these words unto me: I will multiply thee, and thy seed after thee,[u] like unto these; and if thou canst count the number of sands, so shall be the number of thy seeds.

15. And the Lord said unto me: Abraham, I show these things unto thee before ye go into Egypt, that ye may declare all these words.

16. If two things exist,[v] and there be one above the other, there shall be greater things above them;[w] therefore Kolob[x] is the greatest of all the Kokaubeam[y] that thou hast seen, because it is nearest unto me.

17. Now, if there be two things, one above the other, and the moon be above the earth, then it may be that a planet or a star may exist above it; and there is nothing that the Lord thy God shall take in his heart to do but what he will do it.

18. Howbeit that he made the greater star; as, also, if there be two spirits, and one shall be more intelligent than the other, yet these two spirits, notwithstanding one is more intelligent than the other, have no beginning; they existed before, they shall have no end, they shall exist after, for they are gnolaum, or eternal.[z]

19. And the Lord said unto me: These two facts do exist,[2a] that there are two spirits, one being more intelligent than the other; there shall be another more intelligent than they; I am the Lord thy God, I am more intelligent than they all.

20. The Lord thy God sent his angel to deliver thee from the hands of the priest of Elkenah.[2b]

21. I dwell in the midst of them all; I now, therefore, have come down unto thee to deliver unto thee the works which my hands have made,[2c] wherein my wisdom excelleth them all, for I rule in the heavens above, and in the earth beneath, in all wisdom and prudence, over all the intelligences[2d] thine eyes have seen from the beginning; I came down in the beginning in the midst of all the intelligences thou hast seen.

22. Now the Lord had shown unto me, Abraham, the intelligences[2e] that were organized before the world was; and among all these there were many of the noble and great ones;

23. And God saw these souls that they were good, and he stood in the midst of them, and he said: These I will make my rulers; for he stood among those that were spirits,[2f] and he saw that they were good; and he said unto me: Abraham, thou art one of them; thou wast chosen[2g] before thou wast born.

24. And there stood one among them that was like unto God,[2h] and he said unto those who were with him: We will go down, for there is space there, and we will

s, compare Moses 1:4. 7:30.   t, ver. 16.   u, 2:9.   v, ver. 6.   w, compare ver. 8.   x, ver. 3.   y, ver. 13.   z, compare D. & C. 93:23, 29.   2a, ver. 6.   2b, 1:15.   2c, ver. 11.   2d, ver. 22.   2e, ver. 21.   2f, compare Moses 3:5.   2g, see Moses 1:25.   2h, compare Moses 2:1.

take of these materials, and we will make an earth whereon these may dwell;

25. And we will prove them herewith, to see if they will do all things whatsoever the Lord their God shall command them;

26. And they who keep their first estate shall be added upon; and they who keep not their first estate shall not have glory in the same kingdom with those who keep their first estate;[2i] and they who keep their second estate shall have glory added upon their heads for ever and ever.

27. And the Lord said: Whom shall I send? And one answered like unto the Son of Man: Here am I, send me. And another answered and said: Here am I, send me.[2j] And the Lord said: I will send the first.

28. And the second was angry,[2k] and kept not his first estate;[2l] and, at that day, many followed after him.

CHAPTER 4.[a]

1. And then the Lord said: Let us go down. And they went down at the beginning, and they, that is the Gods, organized and formed the heavens and the earth.

2. And the earth, after it was formed, was empty and desolate, because they had not formed anything but the earth; and darkness reigned upon the face of the deep, and the Spirit of the Gods was brooding upon the face of the waters.

3. And they (the Gods) said: Let there be light; and there was light.

4. And they (the Gods) comprehended the light, for it was bright; and they divided the light, or caused it to be divided, from the darkness.

5. And the Gods called the light Day, and the darkness they called Night. And it came to pass that from the evening until morning they called night; and from the morning until the evening they called day; and this was the first, or the beginning, of that which they called day and night.[b]

6. And the Gods also said: Let there be an expanse in the midst of the waters, and it shall divide the waters from the waters.

7. And the Gods ordered the expanse, so that it divided the waters which were under the expanse from the waters which were above the expanse; and it was so, even as they ordered.[c]

8. And the Gods called the expanse, Heaven. And it came to pass that it was from evening until morning that they called night; and it came to pass that it was from morning until evening that they called day; and this was the second time that they called night and day.[d]

9. And the Gods ordered, saying: Let the waters under the heaven be gathered together unto one place, and let the earth come up dry; and it was so as they ordered;

10. And the Gods pronounced the dry land, earth; and the gathering together of the waters, pronounced they, great waters; and the Gods saw that they were obeyed.[e]

11. And the Gods said: Let us prepare the earth to bring forth grass; the herb yielding seed; the fruit tree yielding fruit, after his kind, whose seed in itself yieldeth its own likeness upon the

---

2i, compare ver. 28. Jude 6   2j, see Moses 4:1—2.   2k, Moses 4:3. 2l, ver. 26.   CHAP. 4: a, compare verse by verse with Moses chap. 2, and Gen. chap. 1.   b, compare vers. 8, 13, 19, 23, 31. 5:2, 3.   c, compare vers. 9, 10, 11, 12, 21, 24, 25, 31.   d, see ver. 5.   e, see ver. 7.

earth; and it was so, even as they ordered.*f*

12. And the (Gods) organized the earth to bring forth grass from its own seed, and the herb to bring forth herb from its own seed, yielding seed after his kind; and the earth to bring forth the tree from its own seed, yielding fruit, whose seed could only bring forth the same in itself, after his kind; and the Gods saw that they were obeyed.*g*

13. And it came to pass that they numbered the days; from the evening until the morning they called night; and it came to pass, from the morning until the evening they called day; and it was the third time.*h*

14. And the (Gods) organized the lights in the expanse of the heaven, and caused them to divide the day from the night; and organized them to be for signs and for seasons, and for days and for years;

15. And organized them to be for lights in the expanse of the heaven to give light upon the earth; and it was so.

16. And the (Gods) organized the two great lights, the greater light to rule the day, and the lesser light to rule the night; with the lesser light they set the stars also;

17. And the (Gods) set them in the expanse of the heavens, to give light upon the earth, and to rule over the day and over the night, and to cause to divide the light from the darkness.

18. And the Gods watched those things which they had ordered until they obeyed.

19. And it came to pass that it was from evening until morning that it was night; and it came to pass that it was from morning until evening that it was day; and it was the fourth time.*i*

20. And the (Gods) said: Let us prepare the waters to bring forth abundantly the moving creatures that have life; and the fowl, that they may fly above the earth in the open expanse of heaven.

21. And the (Gods) prepared the waters that they might bring forth great whales, and every living creature that moveth, which the waters were to bring forth abundantly after their kind; and every winged fowl after their kind. And the (Gods) saw that they would be obeyed,*j* and that their plan was good.

22. And the (Gods) said: We will bless them, and cause them to be fruitful and multiply, and fill the waters in the seas or great waters; and cause the fowl to multiply in the earth.

23. And it came to pass that it was from evening until morning that they called night; and it came to pass that it was from morning until evening that they called day; and it was the fifth time.*k*

24. And the (Gods) prepared the earth to bring forth the living creature after his kind, cattle and creeping things, and beasts of the earth after their kind; and it was so, as they had said.*l*

25. And the (Gods) organized the earth to bring forth the beasts after their kind, and cattle after their kind, and every thing that creepeth upon the earth after its kind; and the (Gods) saw they would obey.*m*

26. And the Gods took counsel among themselves and said: Let us go down and form man in our

f, see ver. 7.   g, see ver. 7.   h, see ver. 5.   i, see ver. 5.   j, see ver. 7.
k, see ver. 5.   l, see ver. 7.   m, see ver. 7.

image, after our likeness; and we will give them dominion over the fish of the sea, and over the fowl of the air, and over the cattle, and over all the earth, and over every creeping thing that creepeth upon the earth.

27. So the Gods went down to organize man in their own image, in the image of the Gods to form they him, male and female to form they them.

28. And the Gods said: We will bless them. And the Gods said: We will cause them to be fruitful, and multiply, and replenish the earth, and subdue it, and to have dominion over the fish of the sea, and over the fowl of the air, and over every living thing that moveth upon the earth.

29. And the Gods said: Behold, we will give them every herb bearing seed that shall come upon the face of all the earth, and every tree which shall have fruit upon it; yea, the fruit of the tree yielding seed to them we will give it; it shall be for their meat.

30. And to every beast of the earth, and to every fowl of the air, and to every thing that creepeth upon the earth, behold, we will give them life, and also we will give to them every green herb for meat, and all these things shall be thus organized.

31. And the Gods said: We will do everything that we have said, and organize them; and behold, they shall be very obedient.[n] And it came to pass that it was from evening until morning they called night; and it came to pass that it was from morning until evening that they called day;[o] and they numbered the sixth time.[p]

CHAPTER 5.

1.[a] And thus we will finish the heavens and the earth, and all the hosts of them.

2. And the Gods said among themselves: On the seventh time[b] we will end our work, which we have counseled; and we will rest on the seventh time from all our work which we have counseled.

3. And the Gods concluded upon the seventh time,[c] because that on the seventh time they would rest from all their works which they (the Gods) counseled among themselves to form; and sanctified it. And thus were their decisions at the time that they counseled among themselves to form the heavens and the earth.

4. And the Gods came down and formed these the generations of the heavens and of the earth, when they were formed in the day that the Gods formed the earth and the heavens,

5. According to all that which they had said concerning every plant of the field before it was in the earth, and every herb of the field before it grew; for the Gods had not caused it to rain upon the earth when they counseled to do them, and had not formed a man to till the ground.

6. But there went up a mist from the earth, and watered the whole face of the ground.

7. And the Gods formed man from the dust of the ground, and took his spirit (that is, the man's spirit), and put it into him; and breathed into his nostrils the breath of life, and man became a living soul.

8. And the Gods planted a garden, eastward in Eden, and

---

n, see ver. 7.   **o,** see ver. 5.   **p,** compare chap. 4, verse by verse, with Moses chap. 2, and with Gen. chap. 1.   CHAP. 5: **a,** compare vers. 1—10 with corresponding verses of Moses chap. 3, and Gen. chap. 2.   **b,** see ver. 3. Compare 3:5.   **c,** see ver. 2.

there they put the man, whose spirit they had put into the body which they had formed.

9. And out of the ground made the Gods to grow every tree that is pleasant to the sight and good for food; the tree of life, also, in the midst of the garden, and the tree of knowledge of good and evil.

10. There was a river running out of Eden, to water the garden, and from thence it was parted and became into four heads.*d*

11.*e* And the Gods took the man and put him in the Garden of Eden, to dress it and to keep it.

12. And the Gods commanded the man, saying: Of every tree of the garden thou mayest freely eat,

13. But of the tree of knowledge of good and evil, thou shalt not eat of it; for in the time that thou eatest thereof, thou shalt surely die. Now I, Abraham, saw that it was after the Lord's time,*f* which was after the time of Kolob;*g* for as yet the Gods had not appointed unto Adam his reckoning.

14. And the Gods said: Let us make an help meet for the man, for it is not good that the man should be alone, therefore we will form an help meet for him.*h*

15.*i* And the Gods caused a deep sleep to fall upon Adam; and he slept, and they took one of his ribs, and closed up the flesh in the stead thereof;

16. And of the rib which the Gods had taken from man, formed they a woman, and brought her unto the man.

17. And Adam said: This was bone of my bones, and flesh of my flesh; now she shall be called Woman, because she was taken out of man;

18. Therefore shall a man leave his father and his mother, and shall cleave unto his wife, and they shall be one flesh.

19. And they were both naked, the man and his wife, and were not ashamed.*j*

20.*k* And out of the ground the Gods formed every beast of the field, and every fowl of the air, and brought them unto Adam to see what he would call them; and whatsoever Adam called every living creature, that should be the name thereof.

21. And Adam gave names to all cattle, to the fowl of the air, to every beast of the field; and for Adam, there was found an help meet for him.

d, compare verses 1—10 with corresponding verses of Moses chap. 3, and Gen. chap. 2. e, compare vers. 11—14 with Moses 3:15—18, and Gen. 2:15—18. f, compare 3:4. g, 3:3. h, see ver. 21. i, compare vers. 15—19 with Moses 3:21—25, and Gen. 2:21—25. j, see ver. 15. k, compare vers. 20, 21 with Moses 3:19, 20, and with Gen. 2:19, 20.

A FACSIMILE FROM THE BOOK OF ABRAHAM

No. 3.

EXPLANATION OF THE ABOVE CUT.

1. Abraham sitting upon Pharaoh's throne, by the politeness of the king, with a crown upon his head, representing the Priesthood, as emblematical of the grand Presidency in Heaven; with the scepter of justice and judgment in his hand.

2. King Pharaoh, whose name is given in the characters above his head.

3. Signifies Abraham in Egypt—referring to Abraham, as given in the ninth number of the *Times and Seasons*. (Also as given in the first facsimile of this book.)

4. Prince of Pharaoh, King of Egypt, as written above the hand.

5. Shulem, one of the king's principal waiters, as represented by the characters above his hand.

6. Olimlah, a slave belonging to the prince.

Abraham is reasoning upon the principles of Astronomy, in the king's court.

WRITINGS OF JOSEPH SMITH

1.

AN EXTRACT FROM A TRANSLATION OF THE BIBLE

Being the twenty-fourth chapter of Matthew, commencing with the last verse of the twenty-third chapter, King James' Version.

1. For I say unto you, that ye shall not see me henceforth and know that I am he of whom it is written by the prophets, until ye shall say: Blessed is he who cometh in the name of the Lord, in the clouds of heaven, and all the holy angels with him. Then understood his disciples that he should come again on the earth, after that he was glorified and crowned on the right hand of God.

2. And Jesus went out, and departed from the temple; and his disciples came to him, for to hear him, saying: Master, show us concerning the buildings of the temple, as thou hast said—They shall be thrown down, and left unto you desolate.

3. And Jesus said unto them: See ye not all these things, and do ye not understand them? Verily I say unto you, there shall not be left here, upon this temple, one stone upon another that shall not be thrown down.

4. And Jesus left them, and went upon the Mount of Olives. And as he sat upon the Mount of Olives, the disciples came unto him privately, saying: Tell us when shall these things be which thou hast said concerning the destruction of the temple, and the Jews; and what is the sign of thy coming, and of the end of the world, or the destruction of the wicked, which is the end of the world?

5. And Jesus answered, and said unto them: Take heed that no man deceive you;

6. For many shall come in my name, saying—I am Christ—and shall deceive many;

7. Then shall they deliver you up to be afflicted, and shall kill you, and ye shall be hated of all nations, for my name's sake;

8. And then shall many be offended, and shall betray one another;

9. And many false prophets shall arise, and shall deceive many;

10. And because iniquity shall abound, the love of many shall wax cold;

11. But he that remaineth steadfast and is not overcome, the same shall be saved.

12. When you, therefore, shall see the abomination of desolation, spoken of by Daniel the prophet, concerning the destruction of Jerusalem, then you shall stand in the holy place; whoso readeth let him understand.

13. Then let them who are in Judea flee into the mountains;

14. Let him who is on the housetop flee, and not return to take anything out of his house;

15. Neither let him who is in the field return back to take his clothes;

16. And wo unto them that are with child, and unto them that give suck in those days;

17. Therefore, pray ye the Lord that your flight be not in the winter, neither on the Sabbath day;

18. For then, in those days, shall be great tribulation on the Jews, and upon the inhabitants of Jerusalem, such as was not before sent upon Israel, of God, since the beginning of their kingdom until this time; no, nor ever shall be sent again upon Israel.

19. All things which have befallen them are only the beginning of the sorrows which shall come upon them.

20. And except those days should be shortened, there should none of their flesh be saved; but for the elect's sake, according to the covenant, those days shall be shortened.

21. Behold, these things I have spoken unto you concerning the Jews; and again, after the tribulation of those days which shall come upon Jerusalem, if any man shall say unto you, Lo, here is Christ, or there, believe him not;

22. For in those days there shall also arise false Christs, and false prophets, and shall show great signs and wonders, insomuch, that, if possible, they shall deceive the very elect, who are the elect according to the covenant.

23. Behold, I speak these things unto you for the elect's sake; and you also shall hear of wars, and rumors of wars; see that ye be not troubled, for all I have told you must come to pass; but the end is not yet.

24. Behold, I have told you before;

25. Wherefore, if they shall say unto you: Behold, he is in the desert; go not forth; Behold, he is in the secret chambers; believe it not;

26. For as the light of the morning cometh out of the east, and shineth even unto the west, and covereth the whole earth, so shall also the coming of the Son of Man be.

27. And now I show unto you a parable. Behold, wheresoever the carcass is, there will the eagles be gathered together; so likewise shall mine elect be gathered from the four quarters of the earth.

28. And they shall hear of wars, and rumors of wars.

29. Behold I speak for mine elect's sake; for nation shall rise against nation, and kingdom against kingdom; there shall be famines, and pestilences, and earthquakes, in divers places.

30. And again, because iniquity shall abound, the love of many shall wax cold; but he that shall not be overcome, the same shall be saved.

31. And again, this Gospel of the Kingdom shall be preached in all the world, for a witness unto all nations, and then shall the end come, or the destruction of the wicked;

32. And again shall the abomination of desolation, spoken of by Daniel the prophet, be fulfilled.

33. And immediately after the tribulation of those days, the sun shall be darkened, and the moon shall not give her light, and the stars shall fall from heaven, and the powers of heaven shall be shaken.

34. Verily, I say unto you, this generation, in which these things shall be shown forth, shall not pass away until all I have told you shall be fulfilled.

35. Although, the days will come, that heaven and earth shall pass away; yet my words shall not pass away, but all shall be fulfilled.

36. And, as I said before, after the tribulation of those days, and the powers of the heavens shall be shaken, then shall appear the sign of the Son of Man in heaven, and then shall all the tribes of the earth mourn; and they shall see the Son of Man coming in the clouds of heaven, with power and great glory;

37. And whoso treasureth up my word, shall not be deceived, for the Son of Man shall come, and he shall send his angels before him with the great sound of a trumpet, and they shall gather together the remainder of his elect from the four winds, from one end of heaven to the other.

38. Now learn a parable of the fig-tree—When its branches are yet tender, and it begins to put forth leaves, you know that summer is nigh at hand;

39. So likewise, mine elect, when they shall see all these things, they shall know that he is near, even at the doors;

40. But of that day, and hour, no one knoweth; no, not the angels of God in heaven, but my Father only.

41. But as it was in the days of Noah, so it shall be also at the coming of the Son of Man;

42. For it shall be with them, as it was in the days which were before the flood; for until the day that Noah entered into the ark they were eating and drinking, marrying and giving in marriage;

43. And knew not until the flood came, and took them all away; so shall also the coming of the Son of Man be.

44. Then shall be fulfilled that which is written, that in the last days, two shall be in the field, the one shall be taken, and the other left;

45. Two shall be grinding at the mill, the one shall be taken, and the other left;

46. And what I say unto one, I say unto all men; watch, therefore, for you know not at what hour your Lord doth come.

47. But know this, if the good man of the house had known in what watch the thief would come, he would have watched, and would not have suffered his house to have been broken up, but would have been ready.

48. Therefore be ye also ready, for in such an hour as ye think not, the Son of Man cometh.

49. Who, then, is a faithful and wise servant, whom his lord hath made ruler over his household, to give them meat in due season?

50. Blessed is that servant whom his lord, when he cometh, shall find so doing; and verily I say unto you, he shall make him ruler over all his goods.

51. But if that evil servant shall say in his heart: My lord delayeth his coming,

52. And shall begin to smite his fellow-servants, and to eat and drink with the drunken,

53. The lord of that servant shall come in a day when he looketh not for him, and in an hour that he is not aware of,

54. And shall cut him asunder, and shall appoint him his portion with the hypocrites; there shall be weeping and gnashing of teeth.

55. And thus cometh the end of the wicked, according to the prophecy of Moses, saying: They shall be cut off from among the people; but the end of the earth is not yet, but by and by.

2.

EXTRACTS FROM THE HISTORY OF JOSEPH SMITH, THE PROPHET[a]

1. Owing to the many reports which have been put in circulation by evil-disposed and designing persons, in relation to the rise and progress of the Church of Jesus Christ of Latter-day Saints, all of which have been designed by the authors thereof to militate against its character as a Church and its progress in the world—I have been induced to write this history, to disabuse the public mind, and put all inquirers after truth in possession of the facts, as they have transpired, in relation both to myself and the Church, so far as I have such facts in my possession.

2. In this history I shall present the various events in relation to this Church, in truth and righteousness, as they have transpired, or as they at present exist, being now the eighth year since the organization of the said Church.

3. I was born in the year of our Lord one thousand eight hundred and five, on the twenty-third day of December, in the town of Sharon, Windsor county, State of Vermont. . . . . My father, Joseph Smith, Sen., left the State of Vermont, and moved to Palmyra, Ontario (now Wayne) county, in the State of New York, when I was in my tenth year, or thereabouts. In about four years after my father's arrival in Palmyra, he moved with his family into Manchester, in the same county of Ontario—

4. His family consisting of eleven souls, namely, my father, Joseph Smith; my mother, Lucy Smith (whose name, previous to her marriage, was Mack, daughter of Solomon Mack); my brothers, Alvin (who died November 19th, 1824, in the 27th year of his age), Hyrum, myself, Samuel Harrison, William, Don Carlos; and my sisters, Sophronia, Catherine, and Lucy.

5. Some time in the second year after our removal to Manchester, there was in the place where we lived an unusual excitement on the subject of religion. It commenced with the Methodists, but soon became general among all the sects in that region of country. Indeed, the whole district of country seemed affected by it, and great multitudes united themselves to the different religious parties, which created no small stir and division amongst the people, some crying, "Lo, here!" and others, "Lo, there!" Some were contending for the Methodist faith, some for the Presbyterian, and some for the Baptist.

6. For, notwithstanding the great love which the converts to these different faiths expressed at the time of their conversion, and the great zeal manifested by the respective clergy, who were active in getting up and promoting this extraordinary scene of religious feeling, in order to have everybody converted, as they were pleased to call it, let them join what sect they pleased; yet when the converts began to file off, some to one party and some to

---

a, For the complete record see History of the Church, vol. 1, chaps. 1 to 5 inclusive.

another, it was seen that the seemingly good feelings of both the priests and the converts were more pretended than real; for a scene of great confusion and bad feeling ensued——priest contending against priest, and convert against convert; so that all their good feelings one for another, if they ever had any, were entirely lost in a strife of words and a contest about opinions.

7. I was at this time in my fifteenth year. My father's family was proselyted to the Presbyterian faith, and four of them joined that church, namely, my mother, Lucy; my brothers Hyrum and Samuel Harrison; and my sister Sophronia.

8. During this time of great excitement my mind was called up to serious reflection and great uneasiness; but though my feelings were deep and often poignant, still I kept myself aloof from all these parties, though I attended their several meetings as often as occasion would permit. In process of time my mind became somewhat partial to the Methodist sect, and I felt some desire to be united with them; but so great were the confusion and strife among the different denominations, that it was impossible for a person young as I was, and so unacquainted with men and things, to come to any certain conclusion who was right and who was wrong.

9. My mind at times was greatly excited, the cry and tumult were so great and incessant. The Presbyterians were most decided against the Baptists and Methodists, and used all the powers of both reason and sophistry to prove their errors, or, at least, to make the people think they were in error. On the other hand, the Baptists and Methodists in their turn were equally zealous in endeavoring to establish their own tenets and disprove all others.

10. In the midst of this war of words and tumult of opinions, I often said to myself: What is to be done? Who of all these parties are right; or, are they all wrong together? If any one of them be right, which is it, and how shall I know it?

11. While I was laboring under the extreme difficulties caused by the contests of these parties of religionists, I was one day reading the Epistle of James, first chapter and fifth verse, which reads: *If any of you lack wisdom, let him ask of God, that giveth to all men liberally, and upbraideth not; and it shall be given him.*

12. Never did any passage of scripture come with more power to the heart of man than this did at this time to mine. It seemed to enter with great force into every feeling of my heart. I reflected on it again and again, knowing that if any person needed wisdom from God, I did; for how to act I did not know, and unless I could get more wisdom than I then had, I would never know; for the teachers of religion of the different sects understood the same passages of scripture so differently as to destroy all confidence in settling the question by an appeal to the Bible.

13. At length I came to the conclusion that I must either remain in darkness and confusion, or else I must do as James directs, that is, ask of God. I at length came to the determination to "ask of God," concluding that if he gave wisdom to them that lacked wisdom, and would give

Never??

liberally, and not upbraid, I might venture.

14. So, in accordance with this, my determination to ask of God, I retired to the woods to make the attempt. It was on the morning of a beautiful, clear day, early in the spring of eighteen hundred and twenty. It was the first time in my life that I had made such an attempt, for amidst all my anxieties I had never as yet made the attempt to pray vocally.

15. After I had retired to the place where I had previously designed to go, having looked around me, and finding myself alone, I kneeled down and began to offer up the desires of my heart to God. I had scarcely done so, when immediately I was seized upon by some power which entirely overcame me, and had such an astonishing influence over me as to bind my tongue so that I could not speak. Thick darkness gathered around me, and it seemed to me for a time as if I were doomed to sudden destruction.

16. But, exerting all my powers to call upon God to deliver me out of the power of this enemy which had seized upon me, and at the very moment when I was ready to sink into despair and abandon myself to destruction— not to an imaginary ruin, but to the power of some actual being from the unseen world, who had such marvelous power as I had never before felt in any being— just at this moment of great alarm, I saw a pillar of light exactly over my head, above the brightness of the sun, which descended gradually until it fell upon me.

17. It no sooner appeared than I found myself delivered from the enemy which held me bound.

When the light rested upon me I saw two Personages, whose brightness and glory defy all description, standing above me in the air. One of them spake unto me, calling me by name, and said, pointing to the other—*This is My Beloved Son. Hear Him!*

18. My object in going to inquire of the Lord was to know which of all the sects was right, that I might know which to join. No sooner, therefore, did I get possession of myself, so as to be able to speak, than I asked the Personages who stood above me in the light, which of all the sects was right—and which I should join.

19. I was answered that I must join none of them, for they were all wrong; and the Personage who addressed me said that all their creeds were an abomination in his sight; that those professors were all corrupt; that: "they draw near to me with their lips, but their hearts are far from me; they teach for doctrines the commandments of men, having a form of godliness, but they deny the power thereof."

20. He again forbade me to join with any of them; and many other things did he say unto me, which I cannot write at this time. When I came to myself again, I found myself lying on my back, looking up into heaven. When the light had departed, I had no strength; but soon recovering in some degree, I went home. And as I leaned up to the fireplace, mother inquired what the matter was. I replied, "Never mind, all is well—I am well enough off." I then said to my mother, "I have learned for myself that Presbyterianism is not true." It seems as though the adversary was aware, at a very early period of

COL

my life, that I was destined to prove a disturber and an annoyer of his kingdom; else why should the powers of darkness combine against me? Why the opposition and persecution that arose against me, almost in my infancy?

21. Some few days after I had this vision, I happened to be in company with one of the Methodist preachers, who was very active in the before mentioned religious excitement; and, conversing with him on the subject of religion, I took occasion to give him an account of the vision which I had had. I was greatly surprised at his behavior; he treated my communication not only lightly, but with great contempt, saying it was all of the devil, that there were no such things as visions or revelations in these days; that all such things had ceased with the apostles, and that there would never be any more of them.

22. I soon found, however, that my telling the story had excited a great deal of prejudice against me among professors of religion, and was the cause of great persecution, which continued to increase; and though I was an obscure boy, only between fourteen and fifteen years of age, and my circumstances in life such as to make a boy of no consequence in the world, yet men of high standing would take notice sufficient to excite the public mind against me, and create a bitter persecution; and this was common among all the sects—all united to persecute me.

23. It caused me serious reflection then, and often has since, how very strange it was that an obscure boy, of a little over fourteen years of age, and one, too, who was doomed to the necessity of obtaining a scanty maintenance by his daily labor, should be thought a character of sufficient importance to attract the attention of the great ones of the most popular sects of the day, and in a manner to create in them a spirit of the most bitter persecution and reviling. But strange or not, so it was, and it was often the cause of great sorrow to myself.

24. However, it was nevertheless a fact that I had beheld a vision. I have thought since, that I felt much like Paul,[b] when he made his defense before King Agrippa, and related the account of the vision he had when he saw a light, and heard a voice; but still there were but few who believed him; some said he was dishonest, others said he was mad; and he was ridiculed and reviled. But all this did not destroy the reality of his vision. He had seen a vision, he knew he had, and all the persecution under heaven could not make it otherwise; and though they should persecute him unto death, yet he knew, and would know to his latest breath, that he had both seen a light and heard a voice speaking unto him, and all the world could not make him think or believe otherwise.

25. So it was with me. I had actually seen a light, and in the midst of that light I saw two Personages, and they did in reality speak to me; and though I was hated and persecuted for saying that I had seen a vision, yet it was true; and while they were persecuting me, reviling me, and speaking all manner of evil against me falsely for so saying, I was led to say in my heart: Why persecute me for telling the truth? I have actually seen a vision; and

b, See Acts, chap. 26.

who am I that I can withstand God, or why does the world think to make me deny what I have actually seen? For I had seen a vision; I knew it, and I knew that God knew it, and I could not deny it, neither dared I do it; at least I knew that by so doing I would offend God, and come under condemnation.

26. I had now got my mind satisfied so far as the sectarian world was concerned—that it was not my duty to join with any of them, but to continue as I was until further directed. I had found the testimony of James to be true —that a man who lacked wisdom might ask of God, and obtain, and not be upbraided.

27. I continued to pursue my common vocations in life until the twenty-first of September, one thousand eight hundred and twenty-three, all the time suffering severe persecution at the hands of all classes of men, both religious and irreligious, because I continued to affirm that I had seen a vision.

28. During the space of time which intervened between the time I had the vision and the year eighteen hundred and twenty-three—having been forbidden to join any of the religious sects of the day, and being of very tender years, and persecuted by those who ought to have been my friends and to have treated me kindly, and if they supposed me to be deluded to have endeavored in a proper and affectionate manner to have reclaimed me—I was left to all kinds of temptations; and, mingling with all kinds of society, I frequently fell into many foolish errors, and displayed the weakness of youth, and the foibles of human nature; which, I am sorry to say, led me into divers temptations, offensive in the sight of God. In making this confession, no one need suppose me guilty of any great or malignant sins. A disposition to commit such was never in my nature. But I was guilty of levity, and sometimes associated with jovial company, etc., not consistent with that character which ought to be maintained by one who was called of God as I had been. But this will not seem very strange to any one who recollects my youth, and is acquainted with my native cheery temperament.

29. In consequence of these things, I often felt condemned for my weakness and imperfections; when, on the evening of the above-mentioned twenty-first of September, after I had retired to my bed for the night, I betook myself to prayer and supplication to Almighty God for forgiveness of all my sins and follies, and also for a manifestation to me, that I might know of my state and standing before him; for I had full confidence in obtaining a divine manifestation, as I previously had one.

30. While I was thus in the act of calling upon God, I discovered a light appearing in my room, which continued to increase until the room was lighter than at noonday, when immediately a personage appeared at my bedside, standing in the air, for his feet did not touch the floor.

31. He had on a loose robe of most exquisite whiteness. It was a whiteness beyond anything earthly I had ever seen; nor do I believe that any earthly thing could be made to appear so exceedingly white and brilliant. His hands were naked, and his arms also, a little above the wrist; so, also, were his feet naked, as were

his legs, a little above the ankles. His head and neck were also bare. I could discover that he had no other clothing on but this robe, as it was open, so that I could see into his bosom.

32. Not only was his robe exceedingly white, but his whole person was glorious beyond description, and his countenance truly like lightning. The room was exceedingly light, but not so very bright as immediately around his person. When I first looked upon him, I was afraid; but the fear soon left me.

33. He called me by name, and said unto me that he was a messenger sent from the presence of God to me, and that his name was Moroni; that God had a work for me to do; and that my name should be had for good and evil among all nations, kindreds, and tongues, or that it should be both good and evil spoken of among all people.

34. He said there was a book deposited, written upon gold plates, giving an account of the former inhabitants of this continent, and the source from whence they sprang. He also said that the fulness of the everlasting Gospel was contained in it, as delivered by the Savior to the ancient inhabitants;

35. Also, that there were two stones in silver bows—and these stones, fastened to a breastplate, constituted what is called the Urim and Thummim—deposited with the plates; and the possession and use of these stones were what constituted "seers" in ancient or former times; and that God had prepared them for the purpose of translating the book.

36. After telling me these things, he commenced quoting the prophecies of the Old Testament.

He first quoted part of the third chapter of Malachi; and he quoted also the fourth or last chapter of the same prophecy, though with a little variation from the way it reads in our Bibles. Instead of quoting the first verse as it reads in our books, he quoted it thus:

37. *For behold, the day cometh that shall burn as an oven, and all the proud, yea, and all that do wickedly shall burn as stubble; for they that come shall burn them, saith the Lord of Hosts, that it shall leave them neither root nor branch.*

38. And again, he quoted the fifth verse thus: *Behold, I will reveal unto you the Priesthood, by the hand of Elijah the prophet, before the coming of the great and dreadful day of the Lord.*

39. He also quoted the next verse differently: *And he shall plant in the hearts of the children the promises made to the fathers, and the hearts of the children shall turn to their fathers. If it were not so, the whole earth would be utterly wasted at his coming.*

40. In addition to these, he quoted the eleventh chapter of Isaiah, saying that it was about to be fulfilled. He quoted also the third chapter of Acts, twenty-second and twenty-third verses, precisely as they stand in our New Testament. He said that that prophet was Christ; but the day had not yet come when "they who would not hear his voice should be cut off from among the people," but soon would come.

41. He also quoted the second chapter of Joel, from the twenty-eighth verse to the last. He also said that this was not yet fulfilled, but was soon to be. And he further stated that the fulness of the Gentiles was soon to come

in. He quoted many other passages of scripture, and offered many explanations which cannot be mentioned here.

42. Again, he told me, that when I got those plates of which he had spoken—for the time that they should be obtained was not yet fulfilled—I should not show them to any person; neither the breastplate with the Urim and Thummim; only to those to whom I should be commanded to show them; if I did I should be destroyed. While he was conversing with me about the plates, the vision was opened to my mind that I could see the place where the plates were deposited, and that so clearly and distinctly that I knew the place again when I visited it.

43. After this communication, I saw the light in the room begin to gather immediately around the person of him who had been speaking to me, and it continued to do so until the room was again left dark, except just around him; when, instantly I saw, as it were, a conduit open right up into heaven, and he ascended till he entirely disappeared, and the room was left as it had been before this heavenly light had made its appearance.

44. I lay musing on the singularity of the scene, and marveling greatly at what had been told to me by this extraordinary messenger; when, in the midst of my meditation, I suddenly discovered that my room was again beginning to get lighted, and in an instant, as it were, the same heavenly messenger was again by my bedside.

45. He commenced, and again related the very same things which he had done at his first visit, without the least variation; which having done, he informed me of great judgments which were coming upon the earth, with great desolations by famine, sword, and pestilence; and that these grievous judgments would come on the earth in this generation. Having related these things, he again ascended as he had done before.

46. By this time, so deep were the impressions made on my mind, that sleep had fled from my eyes, and I lay overwhelmed in astonishment at what I had both seen and heard. But what was my surprise when again I beheld the same messenger at my bedside, and heard him rehearse or repeat over again to me the same things as before; and added a caution to me, telling me that Satan would try to tempt me (in consequence of the indigent circumstances of my father's family), to get the plates for the purpose of getting rich. This he forbade me, saying that I must have no other object in view in getting the plates but to glorify God, and must not be influenced by any other motive than that of building his kingdom; otherwise I could not get them.

47. After this third visit, he again ascended into heaven as before, and I was again left to ponder on the strangeness of what I had just experienced; when almost immediately after the heavenly messenger had ascended from me for the third time, the cock crowed, and I found that day was approaching, so that our interviews must have occupied the whole of that night.

48. I shortly after arose from my bed, and, as usual, went to the necessary labors of the day; but, in attempting to work as at other times, I found my strength

so exhausted as to render me entirely unable. My father, who was laboring along with me, discovered something to be wrong with me, and told me to go home. I started with the intention of going to the house; but, in attempting to cross the fence out of the field where we were, my strength entirely failed me, and I fell helpless on the ground, and for a time was quite unconscious of anything.

49. The first thing that I can recollect was a voice speaking unto me, calling me by name. I looked up, and beheld the same messenger standing over my head, surrounded by light as before. He then again related unto me all that he had related to me the previous night, and commanded me to go to my father and tell him of the vision and commandments which I had received.

50. I obeyed; I returned to my father in the field, and rehearsed the whole matter to him. He replied to me that it was of God, and told me to go and do as commanded by the messenger. I left the field, and went to the place where the messenger had told me the plates were deposited; and owing to the distinctness of the vision which I had had concerning it, I knew the place the instant that I arrived there.

51. Convenient to the village of Manchester, Ontario county, New York, stands a hill of considerable size, and the most elevated of any in the neighborhood. On the west side of this hill, not far from the top, under a stone of considerable size, lay the plates, deposited in a stone box. This stone was thick and rounding in the middle on the upper side, and thinner towards the edges, so that the middle part of it was visible above the ground, but the edge all around was covered with earth.

52. Having removed the earth, I obtained a lever, which I got fixed under the edge of the stone, and with a little exertion raised it up. I looked in, and there indeed did I behold the plates, the Urim and Thummim, and the breastplate, as stated by the messenger. The box in which they lay was formed by laying stones together in some kind of cement. In the bottom of the box were laid two stones crossways of the box, and on these stones lay the plates and the other things with them.

53. I made an attempt to take them out, but was forbidden by the messenger, and was again informed that the time for bringing them forth had not yet arrived, neither would it, until four years from that time; but he told me that I should come to that place precisely in one year from that time, and that he would there meet with me, and that I should continue to do so until the time should come for obtaining the plates.

54. Accordingly, as I had been commanded, I went at the end of each year, and at each time I found the same messenger there, and received instruction and intelligence from him at each of our interviews, respecting what the Lord was going to do, and how and in what manner his kingdom was to be conducted in the last days.

55. As my father's worldly circumstances were very limited, we were under the necessity of laboring with our hands, hiring out by day's work and otherwise, as we could get opportunity. Sometimes we were at home, and some-

times abroad, and by continuous labor were enabled to get a comfortable maintenance.

56. In the year 1824 my father's family met with a great affliction by the death of my eldest brother, Alvin. In the month of October, 1825, I hired with an old gentleman by the name of Josiah Stoal, who lived in Chenango county, State of New York. He had heard something of a silver mine having been opened by the Spaniards in Harmony, Susquehanna county, State of Pennsylvania; and had, previous to my hiring to him, been digging, in order, if possible, to discover the mine. After I went to live with him, he took me, with the rest of his hands, to dig for the silver mine, at which I continued to work for nearly a month, without success in our undertaking, and finally I prevailed with the old gentleman to cease digging after it. Hence arose the very prevalent story of my having been a money-digger.

57. During the time that I was thus employed, I was put to board with a Mr. Isaac Hale, of that place; it was there I first saw my wife (his daughter), Emma Hale. On the 18th of January, 1827, we were married, while I was yet employed in the service of Mr. Stoal.

58. Owing to my continuing to assert that I had seen a vision, persecution still followed me, and my wife's father's family were very much opposed to our being married. I was, therefore, under the necessity of taking her elsewhere; so we went and were married at the house of Squire Tarbill, in South Bainbridge, Chenango county, New York. Immediately after my marriage, I left Mr. Stoal's, and went to my father's, and farmed with him that season.

59. At length the time arrived for obtaining the plates, the Urim and Thummim, and the breastplate. On the twenty-second day of September, one thousand eight hundred and twenty-seven, having gone as usual at the end of another year to the place where they were deposited, the same heavenly messenger delivered them up to me with this charge: that I should be responsible for them; that if I should let them go carelessly, or through any neglect of mine, I should be cut off; but that if I would use all my endeavors to preserve them, until he, the messenger, should call for them, they should be protected.

60. I soon found out the reason why I had received such strict charges to keep them safe, and why it was that the messenger had said that when I had done what was required at my hand, he would call for them. For no sooner was it known that I had them, than the most strenuous exertions were used to get them from me. Every stratagem that could be invented was resorted to for that purpose. The persecution became more bitter and severe than before, and multitudes were on the alert continually to get them from me if possible. But by the wisdom of God, they remained safe in my hands, until I had accomplished by them what was required at my hand. When, according to arrangements, the messenger called for them, I delivered them up to him; and he has them in his charge until this day, being the second day of May, one thousand eight hundred and thirty-eight.

61. The excitement, however, still continued, and rumor with her thousand tongues was all the time employed in circulating falsehoods about my father's family, and about myself. If I were to relate a thousandth part of them, it would fill up volumes. The persecution, however, became so intolerable that I was under the necessity of leaving Manchester, and going with my wife to Susquehanna county, in the State of Pennsylvania. While preparing to start—being very poor, and the persecution so heavy upon us that there was no probability that we would ever be otherwise—in the midst of our afflictions we found a friend in a gentleman by the name of Martin Harris, who came to us and gave me fifty dollars to assist us on our journey. Mr. Harris was a resident of Palmyra township, Wayne county, in the State of New York, and a farmer of respectability.

62. By this timely aid was I enabled to reach the place of my destination in Pennsylvania; and immediately after my arrival there I commenced copying the characters off the plates. I copied a considerable number of them, and by means of the Urim and Thummim I translated some of them, which I did between the time I arrived at the house of my wife's father, in the month of December, and the February following.

63. Sometime in this month of February, the aforementioned Mr. Martin Harris came to our place, got the characters which I had drawn off the plates, and started with them to the city of New York. For what took place relative to him and the char-

acters, I refer to his own account of the circumstances, as he related them to me after his return, which was as follows:

64. "I went to the city of New York, and presented the characters which had been translated, with the translation thereof, to Professor Charles Anthon, a gentleman celebrated for his literary attainments. Professor Anthon stated that the translation was correct, more so than any he had before seen translated from the Egyptian. I then showed him those which were not yet translated, and he said that they were Egyptian, Chaldaic, Assyriac, and Arabic; and he said they were true characters. He gave me a certificate, certifying to the people of Palmyra that they were true characters, and that the translation of such of them as had been translated was also correct. I took the certificate and put it into my pocket, and was just leaving the house, when Mr. Anthon called me back, and asked me how the young man found out that there were gold plates in the place where he found them. I answered that an angel of God had revealed it unto him.

65. "He then said to me, 'Let me see that certificate.' I accordingly took it out of my pocket and gave it to him, when he took it and tore it to pieces, saying that there was no such thing now as ministering of angels, and that if I would bring the plates to him he would translate them. I informed him that part of the plates were sealed, and that I was forbidden to bring them. He replied, 'I cannot read a sealed book.' I left him and went to Dr. Mitchell, who sanctioned what Professor Anthon had said re-

specting both the characters and the translation."

. . . . . .

66. On the 5th day of April, 1829, Oliver Cowdery came to my house, until which time I had never seen him. He stated to me that having been teaching school in the neighborhood where my father resided, and my father being one of those who sent to the school, he went to board for a season at his house, and while there the family related to him the circumstance of my having received the plates, and accordingly he had come to make inquiries of me.

67. Two days after the arrival of Mr. Cowdery (being the 7th of April) I commenced to translate the Book of Mormon, and he began to write for me.

68. We still continued the work of translation, when, in the ensuing month (May, 1829), we on a certain day went into the woods to pray and inquire of the Lord respecting baptism for the remission of sins, that we found mentioned in the translation of the plates. While we were thus employed, praying and calling upon the Lord, a messenger from heaven descended in a cloud of light, and having laid his hands upon us, he ordained us, saying:

69. *Upon you my fellow servants, in the name of Messiah, I confer the Priesthood of Aaron, which holds the keys of the ministering of angels, and of the gospel of repentance, and of baptism by immersion for the remission of sins; and this shall never be taken again from the earth until the sons of Levi do offer again an offering unto the Lord in righteousness.*

70. He said this Aaronic Priesthood had not the power of laying on hands for the gift of the Holy Ghost, but that this should be conferred on us hereafter; and he commanded us to go and be baptized, and gave us directions that I should baptize Oliver Cowdery, and that afterwards he should baptize me.

71. Accordingly we went and were baptized. I baptized him first, and afterwards he baptized me—after which I laid my hands upon his head and ordained him to the Aaronic Priesthood, and afterwards he laid his hands on me and ordained me to the same Priesthood—for so we were commanded.

72. The messenger who visited us on this occasion and conferred this Priesthood upon us, said that his name was John, the same that is called John the Baptist in the New Testament, and that he acted under the direction of Peter, James, and John, who held the keys of the Priesthood of Melchizedek, which Priesthood, he said, would in due time be conferred on us, and that I should be called the first Elder of the Church, and he (Oliver Cowdery) the second. It was on the fifteenth day of May, 1829, that we were ordained under the hand of this messenger, and baptized.

73. Immediately on our coming up out of the water after we had been baptized, we experienced great and glorious blessings from our Heavenly Father. No sooner had I baptized Oliver Cowdery, than the Holy Ghost fell upon him, and he stood up and prophesied many things which should shortly come to pass. And again, so soon as I had been baptized by him, I also had the spirit of prophecy, when, standing up, I prophesied concerning the rise of this Church, and many other things connected

with the Church, and this generation of the children of men. We were filled with the Holy Ghost, and rejoiced in the God of our salvation.

74. Our minds being now enlightened, we began to have the scriptures laid open to our understandings, and the true meaning and intention of their more mysterious passages revealed unto us in a manner which we never could attain to previously, nor ever before had thought of. In the meantime we were forced to keep secret the circumstances of having received the Priesthood and our having been baptized, owing to a spirit of persecution which had already manifested itself in the neighborhood.

75. We had been threatened with being mobbed, from time to time, and this, too, by professors of religion. And their intentions of mobbing us were only counteracted by the influence of my wife's father's family (under Divine providence), who had become very friendly to me, and who were opposed to mobs, and were willing that I should be allowed to continue the work of translation without interruption; and therefore offered and promised us protection from all unlawful proceedings, as far as in them lay.

THE ARTICLES OF FAITH

Of The Church of Jesus Christ of Latter-day Saints

1. We believe in God, the Eternal Father, and in His Son, Jesus Christ, and in the Holy Ghost.

2. We believe that men will be punished for their own sins, and not for Adam's transgression.

3. We believe that through the Atonement of Christ, all mankind may be saved, by obedience to the laws and ordinances of the Gospel.

4. We believe that the first principles and ordinances of the Gospel are: first, Faith in the Lord Jesus Christ; second, Repentance; third, Baptism by immersion for the remission of sins; fourth, Laying on of hands for the gift of the Holy Ghost.

5. We believe that a man must be called of God, by prophecy, and by the laying on of hands, by those who are in authority to preach the Gospel and administer in the ordinances thereof.

6. We believe in the same organization that existed in the Primitive Church, viz., apostles, prophets, pastors, teachers, evangelists, etc.

7. We believe in the gift of tongues, prophecy, revelation, visions, healing, interpretation of tongues, etc.

8. We believe the Bible to be the word of God as far as it is translated correctly; we also believe the Book of Mormon to be the word of God.

9. We believe all that God has revealed, all that He does now reveal, and we believe that He will yet reveal many great and important things pertaining to the Kingdom of God.

10. We believe in the literal gathering of Israel and in the restoration of the Ten Tribes; that Zion will be built upon this [the American] continent; that Christ will reign personally upon the earth; and, that the earth will be renewed and receive its paradisiacal glory.

11. We claim the privilege of worshiping Almighty God according to the dictates of our own conscience, and allow all men the same privilege, let them worship how, where, or what they may.

12. We believe in being subject to kings, presidents, rulers, and magistrates, in obeying, honoring, and sustaining the law.

13. We believe in being honest, true, chaste, benevolent, virtuous, and in doing good to all men; indeed, we may say that we follow the admonition of Paul—We believe all things, we hope all things, we have endured many things, and hope to be able to endure all things. If there is anything virtuous, lovely, or of good report or praiseworthy, we seek after these things.—JOSEPH SMITH.

INDEX

Numerals refer to pages and verses. Thus, 11-17 indicates page 11 and verse 17 on that page. In general, the verse in which the beginning of the subject-matter occurs is the only one specified.

5

2-12, 3-19; looked upon Satan; affirms himself a son of God; in similitude of Only Begotten; demands evidence of Satan's glory, 2-13; blesses name of God; judged between God and Satan, 2-15, 18; commands Satan to depart, and deceive not, 2-16; saw bitterness of hell; commanded Satan, 3-20, 21; bore record of visitations of God and Satan, 3-23; called upon God after vanquishment of Satan; blessed and chosen of God; to be made mighty, 3-25; to deliver Israel from bondage, 3-26; inquired of God as to the creation, 3-30; supplicated the Lord for knowledge as to created things, 4-36; commanded to write the words of God, 4-40; to write things revealed to him concerning creation, 4-1.

Mount, in which God spake to Moses, name of not known, 4-42.

Mount Simeon, what Enoch saw and said on, 19-2.

Mountain, Moses caught up into; words of God to Moses in high, 1-1.

Name of the Son, Adam commanded to do all in, 11-8; to be known in the earth forever, 30-19.

Natural Eyes, of Moses could not behold God, 2-11.

Nehor, brother of Abraham, 32-2.

New Jerusalem, called Holy City and Zion, 24-62.

Noah, and posterity foreseen by Enoch, 22-42; to be descendant of Enoch, 25-2; prophesied, 25-16; ordained by the Lord after his own order, 26-19; preaching of, 26-20 to 24; it repented him that God had made man, 26-25; a just man and perfect; and his three sons walked with God, 26-27.

Oath's Sake, Lamech slew Irad for the, 14-50.

Obedient, eternal life given to the, 11-11.

Olea, the moon, 37-13.

Onitah, daughters of, sacrificed to idols, 30-11.

Only Begotten, the Savior, full of grace and truth, 1-6; Moses after similitude of, 1-6, 2-13, 16; Moses commanded to call upon God in name of, 2-17; Satan claimed to be the, 3-19; God created heaven and earth by, 4-33, 1; with the Father from the beginning, 6-26; to come in the meridian of time; prepared from foundation of the world, 14-57.

Ordained, Noah was, by the Lord, 26-19.

Original Guilt, atoned for by the Son of God, 18-54.

Patriarchal Government, after manner of Ham, 31-25.

Patriarchs, records concerning, 31-31.

Perdition, Cain to be called, 12-24.

Persecution of Joseph Smith, following his first vision, 49-22; following his receiving the ancient record, 54-60.

Personages, Heavenly, visited Joseph Smith, 48-17.

Peter, James, and John, directed bestowal of Aaronic Priesthood, 56-72.

Pharaoh, god of, 29-6; priest of, 29-7; king of Egypt, descendant of Ham, 31-21; not eligible to priesthood, 31-27.

Plan of Salvation, unto all men, 19-62.

Plates of Gold, containing ancient records revealed to Joseph Smith, 51-34.

Potiphar's Hill, place of idolatrous altar, 30-10; in Ur of Chaldea, 30-20.

Priesthood, was in beginning, shall be in end of world, 15-7; descended from the fathers, Abraham sought appointment unto, 29-3, 4; received by Abraham from Jehovah, 30-18; records concerning the right of, 31-31.

Priesthood of Aaron, conferred by John the Baptist, 56-69.

Priesthood of Melchizedek, Peter, James, and John hold keys of, 56-72.

Priests, idolatrous, sought Abraham's life, 30-12.

Prison, for those who perish in the floods, 22-38.

Promises, given to Abraham, 32-9.

Prove, we will prove them herewith, 38-25.

Purpose, God's own, in creation of earth and man, 3-31.

Read and Write, children of Adam taught to, 14-6.

Record of Moses, lost because of wickedness of men, 3-23.

Records, preserved in hands of Abraham, 31-31.

Redeemed, as many as will may be, 11-9.

Repent, men everywhere commanded to, 11-14, 17-50, 18-57.

Repentance and Baptism, explained to Adam, 18-53 to 62.

Rest, after tribulations, the earth to, 24-61.

Resurrection, foreseen by Enoch, 23-56; of Christ and of all men, foretold to Enoch, 24-62.

Right of Priesthood, records concerning the, 31-31.

Righteous, The, name of Jesus Christ, 23-45, 47.

Righteousness, to be sent from heaven, 24-62.

Rock of Heaven, Messiah called, 23-53.

Rulers, chosen by the Lord before earthly birth, 37-23.

Sacrifice, similitude of that of the Only Begotten, 11-7; of children to idols, 29-7.

Saints, resurrection of, foreseen by Enoch, 23-56.

Salvation, cometh through Jesus Christ only, 18-52.

Sarai, wife of Abraham, 32-2; called Abraham's sister, 33-22 to 25.

Satan, tempted Moses; called Moses son of man; commanded Moses to worship him, 2-12, 19; commanded by Moses to depart, 2-16, 18; rent upon the earth; claimed to be the Only Begotten, 3-19; wailed, and departed from Moses, 3-21, 22; was from the beginning; offered to redeem all mankind; asked for God's honor, 8-1; sought to destroy agency of man, 8-3, became the devil, father of all lies, 8-4; knew not the mind of God; sought to destroy the world, 9-6; claimed to be a son of God; urged disbelief, 11-13; swore to obey Cain, 12-30.

Saved, believers in the Son to be, 11-15.

Savior, The, delivered gospel to ancient inhabitants of American Continent, 51-34.

Scriptures, quoted by Moroni to Joseph Smith, 51-36.

Second Elder of the Church, Oliver Cowdery to be, 56-72.

Second Estate, glory of keeping the, 38-26.

Secret, administered unto Cain by Satan, 13-49.

Secret Oaths, between Satan and Cain, 12-29 to 31.

Secret Works, death administered because of, 15-15.

Sects, declared to be wrong, 48-19

Seed, of Adam and Eve, 11-11.

Seer, Enoch called a, 17-36.

Serpent, beguiled Eve, 9-6.

Seth, son of Adam, 14-2, 15-10; revelation of God to; offered sacrifice, 14-3.

Seventh Day, God ended work on, blessed it and rested, 6-3.

Shagreel, god of, 29-9.

Shinehah, the sun, 37-13.

Son, God called Moses his, 1-4, 6, 7. See **Only Begotten.**

Son of Man, Satan called Moses, 2-12; is name of Only Begotten, even Jesus Christ, 18-57; Enoch saw day of the coming of, 23-47; foreseen by Enoch upon cross, 23-55; Enoch foresaw ascension of, 24-59; second coming of, foretold to Enoch, 24-60.

Sons and Daughters, born unto Adam and Eve, 10-2.

Sons of God, all may become, 19-68; Noah and his sons so called, 25-13.

Sons of Men, in days of Noah, 25-15.

Soul, see **Living Souls.**

Spirit of God, upon Moses, 2-15; enabled Moses to behold earth and inhabitants, 3-27, 28; will not always strive with man, 26-17.

Spirit of Inspiration, given to write by, 14-5.

Spirits, created by God seen by Enoch, 17-36; without beginning or end, are eternal, 37-18; shown to Abraham, 37-22.

Spirits in Prison, Enoch saw some, redeemed, 24-57.

Spiritual Eyes, Moses beheld God by, 2-11.

Spiritually Created, all things were, 7-5, 7.

Stars, revelation to Abraham concerning, 36-2.

Things, all, bear record of God, 19-63.

Time, reckoning of, with respect to heavenly bodies, 36-4.

Time, Meridian of, see **Meridian of Time.**

Time, The Lord's, manner of reckoning, 36-4, 9.

Torment, those who perish in floods to be in, 22-39.

Transfigured, Moses, was before God, 2-11.

Transgression, because of Adam's, his eyes were opened, 11-10; Adam would not have had seed without; Adam and Eve knew good and evil through, 11-11.

Tree, of life; of knowledge of good and evil, 7-9.

Truth, to be sent forth out of the earth, 24-62.

Unclean Thing, cannot dwell in presence of God, 18-57.

Urim and Thummim, given to Abraham, 33-1; deposited with the ancient plates, 51-35; first seen by Joseph Smith, 53-52; delivered into custody of Joseph Smith, 54-59.

Virgins, sacrificed to idols, 30-11.

Wept, the God of heaven, 21-28.

Wicked, of Enoch's day pleaded for by the Chosen, 22-39.

Woman, created and brought to Adam, 8-22.

Word of God's Power, the Only Begotten Son, 4-32; work of creation accomplished by, 5-5.

Words of God, to Moses in the mount, 1-1, 3; never cease, 1-4; esteemed by men as naught; to be restored, 4-41.

Work and Glory of God, to bring to pass the immortality and eternal life of man, 4-39.

Works of God, no man can behold all, 1-5.

Worlds, without number, 4-33; many have passed away; many stand; innumerable unto man, 4-35.

Write, Moses commanded to, concerning creation, 4-1.

Write and Read, children of Adam taught to, 14-6.

Zion, why the Lord so called his people, 21-18; Enoch built city of, 21-19; taken into heaven, 21-21, 23; taken to the bosom of the Lord, 21-31, 25-69; called Holy City, a New Jerusalem, 24-62; to be the Lord's abode, 24-64.

Zion is Fled, God received Zion unto his own bosom, 25-69.

CPSIA information can be obtained at www.ICGtesting.com
Printed in the USA
LVOW03s1926080515

437783LV00023B/784/P